UNDER THE SKYFLOWER TREE

UNDER THE SKYFLOWER TREE

REFLECTIONS OF A NUN-ENTITY

Mona Castelazo

Foreword by Wilkie Au, Ph.D.

iUniverse, Inc.

New York   Lincoln   Shanghai

UNDER THE SKYFLOWER TREE
Reflections of a Nun-entity

iUniverse books may be ordered through booksellers or by contacting:

iUniverse
2021 Pine Lake Road, Suite 100
Lincoln, NE 68512
www.iuniverse.com
1-800-Authors (1-800-288-4677)

ISBN: 0-595-33664-7

Printed in the United States of America

Dedicated to my parents, "Don" and "Dunnie" (John and Margaret),
whose balance and good humor were always inspiring,
in addition to the fact that they were never easily shocked by anything.

Contents

Foreword xi

One   Original Puzzles 1

Two   From Novice to Teacher 23

Three Many Changes 47

Four   Quandries and Questions 74

Five   Time Out for Answers 94

Six   Coming to My Senses 116

Seven Theories and Beyond 134

Eight "Which Vice is Versa?" 152

Nine   Full Circle 168

Acknowledgments

To the following people who made this book possible, I am deeply grateful: Sr. Kathleen Maier for her careful, patient proofreading and sensitivity to detail; Sr. Guadalupe Moore, whose secretarial assistance and advice were indispensable; Sr. Patricia Foster, who typed the initial copy; Joana Gallo Marsteller for her inspiration and guidance; Wilkie Au for his insight and perceptive criticism; my sister Donna Locati for the artwork; my brother Tom Castelazo for his support; my sister Mary Koppel for her appreciation of my humor; Esther Caiazza and Jules and Esther Sanders for their reading of the book and their helpful comments; and finally the members of my religious congregation for their encouragement.

Foreword

Baron Friedrich von Hugel, who served as Evelyn Underhill's spiritual director for a time, proposed an understanding of holistic or integrated religious development in his *The Mystical Aspect of Religion*, first published in 1925. According to von Hugel, integrated religious development entails developing and nurturing three aspects of religious growth: the institutional, the critical, and the mystical. Like a tripartite bridge, all three aspects will have a "joint presence" in the fully developed religious person's life.

Predominant in childhood, the institutional stage consists in learning from our parents, teachers, and others the fundamentals of the religious faith shared by whatever group we are born into. This stage represents a period of receiving what is handed on as the tradition or wisdom of the community. The critical stage occurs mainly during adolescence, once we have acquired the cognitive ability for abstract thinking. During this phase, religious maturity challenges us to reflect critically on what was taught us in childhood. This critical reflection, often instigating a "crisis of faith," is essential for the personal appropriation (making our own) of what we have been taught. In other words, the questioning that we do in this stage is healthy in that it forces us to make sense of and to analyze logically what we have previously regarded as true, simply on the basis of trusting in some external authority. Finally, the mystical stage calls for the cultivation of an inner life and sensitivity to the world of interior experiences. It requires us to access our feelings and emotions, aspirations and hopes, dreams and desires in order to discover the divine in the concrete experiences of our daily lives.

While she does not mention von Hugel's developmental model, Mona Castelazo's story nicely shows how the institutional, critical, and mystical aspects can be woven into life in a way that contributes to wholeness and holiness. As a child, she was raised in a Catholic family and later, after two years of college, joined the Sisters of St. Joseph of Carondelet, a religious order of women. In both these groups, she developed deep roots in her Catholic faith and benefited from the wisdom handed on in group life. With a solid grounding in the institutional, she, some time in midlife, experienced the full force of the critical and mystical stages kicking in. While acknowledging that her development of the critical and mystical was somewhat delayed by being a nun in the period prior to the changes introduced by Vatican II—a vocation that "required submission and a degree of anonymity"—she nevertheless took on Jung's challenge of integrating her "shadow," i.e. aspects of her personal development that were undeveloped or underdeveloped up to then. Encouraged by Jung, she committed herself to the project of individuation, the process of becoming an "unprecedented self," even while staying a faithful member of her religious group. In her ability to retain a sharp sense of her uniqueness while staying true to the collective identity of a Sister of St. Joseph, she fought off the perennial danger of letting one's unique, personal identity be obliterated by the group's identity. As a nun of over fifty years, she has resisted slipping into being a "non-entity," and, fortunately for us, can share her interesting story of being a "nun-entity."

In this autobiography, told with candor and humor, Mona Castelazo illustrates how the Spirit has shown up in her spiritual journey to bring about personal growth, wisdom and maturity. With a vivid style, she narrates the spiritual journey that transformed her from an inquisitive and precocious young woman growing up in Fresno, California, into a critically-thinking, mature adult who found "regurgitated answers" unacceptable for herself and her students. She writes now as a woman made whole and wise by her lifelong openness to Spirit in all of her life experiences and especially by her transforming encounters with such literary and spiritual figures as Shakespeare, Dante, C. S. Lewis, T. S. Eliot, C. G. Jung, Tolkien, Helen Luke, Robert Bly, Ken Wilber, Madeline L'Engle and others. She is able to effectively share with us the wisdom she has gleaned from her literary mentors because in her intimate engagement with their works, she has fruitfully converted abstract knowledge into heart knowledge. Readers will find in this work much encouragement and support for the spiritual journey of becoming a person in whose life God's Spirit continues to bring wholeness and holiness.

Wilkie Au, Ph.D.
Loyola Marymount University
Los Angeles, California
September 8, 2004

One

Original Puzzles

Original sin always puzzled me. It appeared to be neither "original" nor "sin," strictly speaking. It seemed unoriginal, since all of us experience its effects, being subject to ignorance, suffering, evil, and death. It seemed not to be sin at all, in the ordinary sense of the word, because it is not personally chosen. At least, if I had a choice, I'd rather have something else.

When I was "growing up Catholic," we were taught that original sin was transmitted in some mysterious manner from Adam and Eve to their descendents and eventually to us, through our own parents. Since all people share the same predicament, it might have served as a common bond, but being negative, perhaps it was more like having the same family skeleton in all of our closets. In which case, its very presence might account for the universal tendency of people throughout the ages to make a great display of their differences, rather than to let the secret out.

Because I went to a public grammar school, I attended catechism classes in private homes. I was excited by the large charts that the sister catechists used to reveal the mysteries of God to us in a colorful fashion. When it came to abstract definitions to be memorized, I was less interested. Once I carried on a sub-rosa conversation with the girl sitting next to me while the sister teaching us presented the portion of the lesson to be memorized. She called on me to repeat what she had said, adding, "Can you do two things at once?" I answered correctly, giving

1

her to believe that I *could* do two things at the same time, but I had merely repeated the words; no understanding was required.

After having experienced the dark box of the confessional for the first time, I made my First Communion and returned to the class several weeks later. Sister asked me if I had gone to confession. I said, "Yes." (Didn't she know that?) We had some difficulty in communicating until I finally realized that she meant that I should return to confession regularly. I was dumbfounded! No one had made it clear to me that I had to go through that more than once. It was unfair—I had thought all that was behind me.

When I was very young, my mother asked me why I had done a particularly unacceptable thing. I answered truthfully, "I had a chance at it." The thought that I had to tell on myself regularly in confession seemed to reduce my chances in life. We were taught that God watches everything we do—why tell a priest about something that God had already seen in a more colorful version on "action news"?

I went to confession the first time good naturedly, but became less cooperative about it as time went on. Sometimes I hid when I knew we would be going to church for that purpose. Other times I performed songs and dances on the way over, hoping to lure my mother in a different direction, but we always ended up at the church door in spite of my efforts.

The clearest memory I have of confession during my school days was admitting that I stole a piece of pie off a large dessert cart when I played the violin for a Knights of Columbus dinner. Our musical group wasn't invited to the dinner, but I polished off a slice of cream pie in the kitchen on my way back from the rest room. (I feel free to share this without breaking the seal of confession, but you could not hear this from my confessor with impunity.)

Later in life I learned that the sacrament of penance had been originally intended for serious, scandalous sins, which affected the morals or morale of the community at large. The sinner was to confess and do public penance. (This practice seemed to have been adopted in the last decade of the twentieth century by the executive branch of our national government.)

Telling the truth was a virtue, and deceit a matter for confession, but I learned at an early age that mysterious complexities determined which truths were to be told. Sitting at the family table, I once opened a birthday gift that I hated on sight. Immediately my face gave a truthful response, but I was told to smile and say "Thank you." To my horror, I realized that I was doomed to a life of deceit.

When I expressed an honest dislike for certain vegetables on my plate, my visiting godmother said, "What would you say if I told you that there were starving children in Europe who would be lucky to get those vegetables?" I truthfully answered, "To that, I would say—Hoo, Hoo!" I don't remember her reaction (or my mother's) at that time. However, when we visited a friend of my grandmother's who lived in a small house surrounded by trees in Marin County, my honesty produced a reaction from both my parents and my grandmother. I observed to its owner, "This is a very little house, and you're a very big lady, aren't you?" I was sent back to apologize to her before we got into the car. She seemed even bigger when I had to confront her alone. My parents administered just punishments when necessary, but the ambiguous ones come more readily to mind.

Visiting cousins in Vallejo, I found my way into a bedroom and crawled under a little table. Putting my hand up over the table, I felt some pieces of cardboard that came apart in different shapes as I squeezed them. I couldn't see the top, but the pieces started to fall down, unique in size and color. Most fascinating! I had nothing like this in my room at home. Then one of my cousins came by and called to my aunt, "Look what she's doing!" as if I were engaging in an evil activity. Evidently the jigsaw puzzle that I was dismantling delightedly had taken quite a few hours or days for my cousins to assemble.

I began to feel that original sin had to do with acts that seemed innocent, but were stamped "bad" upon completion. For example, a boy down the street had told me about a girl and boy who had crawled under a bush and performed a strange action that produced a baby. It was the tallest, most ridiculous tale I'd ever heard. I couldn't imagine how or why anyone could have dreamed up such a silly story, much less expected anyone to believe it. I shared it with my father who had a good sense of humor and delighted in incongruities. To my astonishment— and considerable pain—he gave me a quick but effective spank. I wanted to tell him that I hadn't believed the story, but a sudden intuition that there was more significance to it than I had allowed stopped me. Surely not...it couldn't...be...true? Maybe there had been some strange occurrence, a freak accident of nature, that others knew about? But I was given no more enlightenment that day.

Other evidences of my original waywardness began to crop up. I was interested in words and, having learned two new words (from the same boy down the street), I tried them out at the dinner table. My father was from the San Francisco Bay area and always spoke of it as "The City." When I pronounced my newfound contraction, "Frisco," it outdid a four-letter word. Hoping to redeem myself, I asked for the "mouse turd." I hadn't learned the meaning of the second term of the compound, and can't remember if the mustard came my way, but my request certainly provoked attention.

Having a tendency to question everything was another trait of mine that seemed under suspicion. One morning when I was on the floor playing with toy cars, I asked my mother why there weren't any red cars in the world—at that time there weren't. She explained that only fire engines and fire chief's cars could be red. I asked why that was so and the question stumped her. I thought that if someone had decided that only certain cars could be red, someone else could very well change it. It was one of my first experiences of the "they" that decided things that others unquestionably go along with.

Another example of my tendency to wonder took place when we visited my maternal grandmother's house one morning. Sunshine fell on some of the furniture in the bedroom—a stuffed brown armchair, a bedspread. The room had a comfortable, lived-in feeling of everyday life that contrasted with my intuition of a deep mystery behind the existence of the things in the room. I knew others had been there and seen these things before me and would be there again, but how did this all work? How did time work? I had a feeling that the immediacy of the reality of this moment was not looked upon as extraordinary by anyone else in the house. One evening I sat at our dining room table by myself long after it had been cleared of dinner things, bounced my fist on the table and wondered, "Why am I here? Why is this table here?" I was aware that the others in the house didn't seem to be sitting around wondering about existence—at least not their own. Some of them did question *my* existence on occasion as Tommy, my little brother, did when my mother explained to him that she loved all of her children. He was incredulous, "You mean *her* too? But she's so screamy." In retrospect, I think of myself as having been a quiet child, but perhaps memory is partial at best.

One of the effects of the Fall of our first parents is said to be physical suffering. When I was five I was visited by an attack of appendicitis at my birthday party. The doctor came to our house and said I needed an operation. That evening at the hospital I was taken to surgery. As I went under the ether, I imagined a dark little cave with a star man sitting in it, rocking back and forth to the tiny beeps of the machine. When I returned home from my hospital stay, I felt like a "star" myself, being the only kid on the block with an appendectomy scar. I decided to show it to the boys down the street. We went into the small playhouse for the viewing. I was feeling rather special until the top of the playhouse disappeared, and I felt the spanking end of the short arm of the law upon me. My father was a diminutive man, but strong. I learned then that showing off was a bad thing—at least a private showing of private parts. Years later Dr. Seuss wrote a book about Star-Belly Sneeches who felt superior to the other sneeches—those without stars on their bellies. This cautionary tale might save small children today from behaving like the Star Bellies, but I learned the hard way.

My original tendencies certainly did seem to need correction. I did not take to being "nice" readily. Although I distinctly remember my mother's having said, "Some of us are not ladies," she disremembers it. "Disremembers" is one of my recently acquired vocabulary words. I learned it from having questioned the use of the word in a student's paper in one of my English classes. After finding it in a few other papers, I looked it up. I had never seen it in print and am not sure when it came into common usage, but it is in the dictionary. I disremember having seen it elsewhere.

Niceness training began early. One of my earliest lessons took place when a friend of my mother's came to visit. She spoke to me kindly and, in order to show my enthusiasm and friendliness, I kicked off one of my small shoes toward the ceiling. Instead of the appreciation I expected for such a feat, my mother took me into the hallway, closed the door, and told me solemnly that "nice girls" didn't do such things, and that no one thought it was cute or funny. Looking back, I still think it was a more interesting response than saying, "How do you do? How are you?" or other conventional responses. But it was an effective lesson—I haven't kicked a shoe off in greeting since.

As far as ladylike practices, I took a dim view of them—wearing dresses in particular. I always preferred jeans or pants. The one place where dresses definitely had to be worn was at church. Once when my mother was away, I tried to talk my father into letting me wear pants to Mass. I pointed out logically that although he was eager to have me put on a dress, it was easy for him, because he didn't ever have to wear one. He went out of the room to think it over, being a reasonable man. Sitting confidently in my room on the floor, where I had been lamenting my fate, I was taken by surprise when he came back, squeezed into one of my mother's dresses. He thought it was funny. I was not amused.

I still had to wear a dress. When he returned down the hall, I could see that the opening of the back of the dress made a big V and revealed most of his freckled back—he hadn't been able to button it.

My father was a cheerful man and a gourmet cook by hobby. On Sundays he cooked bacon and made pancakes in animal shapes for a fine breakfast after Mass. The process required a liberal sprinkling of flour around the kitchen and the opening of almost all of the cupboard doors. It was taken for granted that part of a woman's role was to serve as a cleanup crew, according to my observations of my mother. We enjoyed eggs, sausages and sometimes doughnuts, maple bars or bear claws—all of which I appreciated with fairly ladylike decorum.

However, the real bear claws that my father was given by a hunter friend were another story. Gourmet cooks seem to think they have to try everything. The cooking of these paws from a real bear resulted in a foul, greasy, penetrative odor, which called forth unladylike comments from me, including a vow that I would never enter the family house again. My resolve finally broke down, but I remember watching the outside of the house from the other side of the street as it got dark and the lights went on.

One special Sunday activity was taking a ride in the country. In early spring the redbud trees blossom in the foothills above Fresno—one of the first signs of spring. There is little else of interest to be seen in the countryside before the leaves return and the wildflowers bloom. At that time of year, my parents liked to drive out and look for the redbuds. Perhaps it was too early in the season on one particular Sunday. In any case, the countryside looked barren to me, the day was overcast and midway through the trip I shouted out in a burst of unniceness, "Take me out of this old dead country!" Perhaps this was the sort of thing to which my brother had referred?

Years later, I was consoled by the thought that evidently C. S. Lewis hadn't valued niceness either. In the third book of his space trilogy, *That Hideous Strength,* he places the villains in operation of an institution called N.I.C.E. In the novel the letters stand for "National Institute of Coordinated Experiments," an organization run by a disembodied head ruled by evil forces. Its purpose was to take control of Earth by capitalizing on a group of scientists who had begun to idolize facts, knowledge and abstraction. The N.I.C.E. people tortured both animals and humans, destroyed the natural countryside, and ruined relationships by turning people against each other through fear and suspicion. All this was said to be done in the name of progress and the good of humanity.

Imagination, rather than abstraction, interested me. I was to become an avid reader, walking to the library regularly to find stories. But sitting trapped in the presence of unsolved problems in arithmetic or trying to draw the hands on endless pages of clocks to learn to tell time, felt to me like N.I.C.E. torture. Mystery and possibility held a fascination for me. Sitting in the backyard on an afternoon when the sky was blue, the sun shining, the grass green, I again felt there must be more behind all of it than what I could see. I felt mysteriously confined. Would I get to see all of it someday? I looked around over the fences next door into empty yards. I couldn't see the neighbors, yet I knew they existed. What were they all doing? In this one moment of time I would never know. What did it all mean? Did all of them sit around wondering too? When I went into the garage and stared at the wall of wooden boards, I knew that there also must be more there than I could see. What if the wall moved aside like a curtain and I could see behind it? At the time of World War II, people were drawing a figure looking over a wall captioned, "Kilroy was here." Following that spirit, I found some chalk and drew a Kilroy, adding footprints going up and down the garage wall. I know I (like Kilroy) was there because the marks are still in that garage. Fortunately, I didn't mention any of these tendencies to anyone, or I might not have been considered to be "all there" myself.

Table manners were part of being nice. I remember frosty mornings in Fresno when I would have preferred to put my hands into the hot cereal rather than eat it, but had learned enough by that time not to try it. At lunch one day, when I had eaten around the outside of an apple, my grandmother inspected it and said, "You missed the best part," indicating the part nearer to the core. I thought that if she considered that to be the best part, she could have it, but politely scrutinized it as if considering her suggestion. All the adults I knew had proper table manners, or at least seemed to know what they were. However, an exception comes to mind. One summer when my Uncle Jim came to lunch, my brother decided to crawl around barefoot under the table. My uncle reached down, caught a dirty bare foot with one hand, and deftly spread butter all over the sole. Delighted with such a display of freedom by an adult, I began to realize what a superior man my uncle was.

Creative projects interested me more than good manners. My sister Donna and I with several neighborhood friends made geranium perfume by submerging geranium leaves in glass jars for long periods of time. It wasn't too successful, but at least it was a ritual we created in praise of the pungent odor of the plant. Experiments with insects, which included intimidating them with my index finger to walk the plank into a jar, demonstrated to me the wonderful defenses God provides for insects—bees in particular.

In one of our group projects, my sister and brother and I delineated the outlines of a pirate ship with the garden hose and sailed off in imaginary forays, keeping my mother busy tying pirate scarves, which came loose during skirmishes on the high seas and had to be tied all over again. My new little sister, Mary, joined the ship as a pirate baby. Later we developed more altruistic community projects, such as filling the red wagon with jars of water and listening for fire engine sirens. Upon hearing one, our emergency fire department would spring into action, hoping to beat the engine to the scene. There turned out to be more hoping than action. We then developed more original schemes that wouldn't duplicate existing agencies. Because we were all good at climbing trees and loved to wear blue jeans, we developed a plan to scare off daytime hoodlums. We cut eyeholes in old bed sheets, rolled them into the cuffs of our jeans, and climbed the trees in the front yard to wait for criminals. Our plan was to quickly don the attack garb and swing down on the villains by surprise. Again, there was more waiting than jumping—many practice swoops, but a dearth of criminals. My theory was that they had heard about us and knew better than to darken the sidewalks of our street.

I enjoyed learning, but going to school had its drawbacks. For one thing, I was not allowed to wear my favorite high-top maroon tennis shoes. For another, I felt like the first grader in the joke, who, when asked about his first day at school responded, "It was okay, but it took up most of my day." I remember looking out from a third grade classroom on the second floor one sunny autumn morning. There was a grocery store on the corner where several old men sat in the sun on a bench by the front door. I envied them. They were free to sit there as long as they liked, or to go into the store and buy a popsicle whenever they wanted to. I began to imagine long years of classroom imprisonment stretching endlessly before me. Fortunately, I didn't know then that I would one day become a teacher, extending that time for the period of another generation.

In the fourth grade, I had a teacher who seemed more interested in eating her lunch than in teaching. She developed an elaborate plan for us to make curtains for the classroom's huge windows. Placing long sheets of butcher paper on the floor, she supplied us with large crayons of the wrong sort, not Crayolas, but greasy ones with a coarse texture that made holes in the paper. While we were on the floor drawing and coloring large grainy flowers and leaves, she lunched leisurely on a number of apples and sandwiches at her desk. It didn't seem to be educational at the time, but the experience introduced me to a teacher whose attitude I later encountered in a number of other "educational settings." Her type of enforced, mindless labor might have served as a punishment for lazy students and teachers in one of the circles of a modern *Inferno*.

The imaginative possibilities surrounding Halloween always excited me. When we drew Halloween pictures at school, I filled mine with as many creatures as I could: pumpkins, cats, bats, goblins, ghosts, skeletons, chains, witches, cauldrons, etc. One of the girls in my class—a nice girl—drew a picture of a very neat house (probably hers). Everything was in order. The porch, railing, roof, were all meticulously drawn with a ruler. The colors were nondescript—white space mostly. Set neatly on the railing of the porch was a conventional jack-o'-lantern—neither small nor large, with a non-expressive face. I was astounded when the teacher put her drawing up and praised it, rather than mine. Where had this teacher been? Didn't she know *anything* about Halloween? But it was a "nice" drawing—mostly of the house. I was sorely disappointed, and once again decided that the price of being nice wasn't worth it.

One Halloween I decided to be Superman. The comic books inspired me. Swinging from the trees and dashing faster than a speeding fire engine to put out fires had given me practice. My mother had a wonderful cape that she received in nurse's training—it was red on one side and blue on the other, just like the one worn by the man of steel. That year my girlfriend held a party in her backyard. When all of us, girls and boys, went into the garage, someone turned off the lights. The girls began screaming—maybe a few boys too—but I was Superman, undaunted by such foolery. I shouted over the din, telling them there was nothing to fear—Superman was here, etc., but they seemed to enjoy the screaming. I had been accused of being screamy earlier in life, but couldn't get into this pretend screaming. Was it one of the many unpleasant things required to qualify as a sensitive female? The next year, to fool people, I wore my hair in braids to a Halloween party. I had never worn braids, and used a mask to enhance the disguise. No one would suspect Superman of coming dressed like a little girl the next Halloween. It worked. Pretending to be a lady wasn't too hard, if it didn't last too long.

I became disenchanted with politics early on. My grandmother and I used to listen to the Lone Ranger over the radio once a week. One evening when we turned it on, a non-Lone Ranger voice informed us that the program would not be heard because Dewey was giving a presidential campaign speech. It was unbelievable to me that an action-packed, imaginative adventure would be preempted for anything less than a major disaster. Surely he could give his old speech some other time! I listened to a little bit of it in a state of shock. What I heard, I later found out, was called jargon—speech that sounded good, but didn't seem to go anywhere or say anything. I thought we should elect a strong silent man of action like the Lone Ranger. This man didn't sound like he could even ride a horse. I never forgave him and would have voted against him, had I been old enough.

During World War II, my parents kept chickens in a homemade chicken house behind the garage, and after the war we children used it as a clubhouse. Having become the leader of the neighborhood projects, I devised a scheme to borrow comic books from the other kids in the neighborhood and start a comic book store, lending the books out for five cents apiece. The mother of the two boys who lived next door got wind of my enterprise, called me to task for capitalizing on her sons' comics, and gave me a slap on the face that sent me running back to the club house to hide. Embarrassed, I stayed in the clubhouse until sundown, so that she couldn't see me crawling back to the house in shame. How humiliating to learn that I had criminal tendencies I hadn't even been aware of. But the store had seemed a good idea at the time—and profitable.

Another revelatory shock came when my sister Donna announced to me that she and her friend, Marilyn, were no longer going to take orders from me as the leader. I was crushed. Hadn't I been a good leader? And somebody had to do it—I was the oldest in the group. In addition to becoming a crook, had I also become a tyrant?

Fortunately, an educational opportunity gave me the chance for creativity outside the neighborhood. There was an orchestra at our grammar school, and when I was in the fifth grade I learned to play the violin. Many people think that playing a musical instrument is a luxurious way to express one's feelings, like getting into a relaxing shower and singing. Some may think that playing provides a pleasant background for engaging in serious thinking, as Matlock does with his ukulele or Sherlock with his violin. Actually, practicing a piece of music is hard work. I once noted in a journal: "The world of music is a noble one, demanding discipline, control, and many long and short hours of painstaking practice, which must be done intelligently and little by little. The most important acquired virtue for a musician is perseverance, prompted by a love of the beautiful." I still find it so.

Even the love of beautiful music doesn't entirely come naturally, but must be cultivated, at least by repeated listening. My parents played classical music on the phonograph and tuned into the Standard Hour on the radio. Eventually I learned to love good music. My godfather sang Irish songs after dinner on occasion. I played along on the violin, developing a love of ballads and folk songs. However, when treated to a concert featuring violinist Yehudi Menuhin, I found myself counting all the windows in the hall—I wasn't up to that yet. I remember one of my college music professors having said, "If you ask the average man in the street if he likes Bach, and the answer is yes, he's either lying or he's studied some music."

I began violin studies hoping that the initial scraping sounds would turn into beautiful music. My first lessons required me to travel on the city bus for the first time by myself to a Sherman Clay music store in downtown Fresno. My teacher was a monosyllabic man who taught me to play "Annie Laurie" and to use violin rosin. A piano teacher later came to our house to teach my sister and brother, since they couldn't carry their instrument around. Her name was Miss Berry. She always wore a gray sweatshirt, a baggy skirt, and a beanie. She seemed ancient.

I was exempt from her clutches, but was asked to be a "guest artist" at the recital, which was held at her home. To our amazement, she had a mother, who met us at the door saying, "Miss Berry is primping." We were further entertained by seeing that Miss Berry had placed newspaper on the benches where we were to sit in our nicely starched, white recital clothes. Two mothers observed that she evidently was growing large onions of some sort under her grand piano. They stifled giggles as the recital began. Near the end, Miss Berry, wearing a nicely starched dress herself for a change, accompanied my rendition of "Humoresque," a title that seems apt in retrospect.

Taking up the violin required an independent focus. In addition to spending hours practicing alone, I became more reflective in general. We had a clothesline in the backyard, one pole of which almost touched the neighbor's fence. I took to spending time sitting up on the pole with my feet on the fence, contemplating life. I considered the fact that we who were in grammar school walked down the street to the left toward our school, whereas the boys and girls going to high school and junior high walked in the opposite direction. Would I ever really walk to the right? How was it that I could imagine it beforehand, or rather, really couldn't imagine it, but could think about what might happen in the future? Of course it did happen. The junior high near us opened a sixth grade, and I left grammar school and walked to the right a year earlier than I expected.

Junior high school was busy and interesting. In addition to basic classes, we were offered cooking, sewing, P.E., languages, art, music appreciation and orchestra. I joined the orchestra and won a record of my choice, "The Triumphal March from Aida," for being able to recognize all the selections in the music appreciation class. I learned to play tennis and how to climb over the fence on Saturday with my girlfriend to use the courts when the door was locked—a vestige of my former criminal tendencies. I experienced some typical adolescent crushes, but had a setback when Richard Casey inadvertently stuck a sharp pencil into my right hand in a burst of playfulness. I haven't seen him since that seventh grade class, but the small piece of graphite is still visible, embedded in my palm.

When I was in the eighth grade, my aunt in the East made dresses for me and my two sisters and sent them for Christmas presents. Although I had been delighted when she had made me a green plaid flannel shirt one year, I was appalled to see that she had made all three of these dresses in exactly the same pattern—one for me, one for my sister a year younger than I, and one for my little sister who was nine years younger. They were very "nice" with puffed sleeves and a ribbon to be tied in a bow at the neck. The material was white with a little flower pattern, but the ribbons were black, which matched my mood when I had to wear the dress. I began to wonder about the connection between an inner disposition and outer approval, but I chose the outer approval, feeling that I was forced into a deceitful acquiescence. In case I were to imagine that I pulled it off successfully, I have only to look at the snapshot my father took of us "three ladies" to detect a definite undercover scowl on my face. Perhaps my father thought the sun caused me to squint, but really I was just screamy inside—it attracted less attention.

My father became a Catholic when I was in junior high school, and we were confirmed on the same day. According to the ritual, I was slapped on the cheek (gently), but this slap was a symbol of virtue, rather than a punishment for wrongdoing as in the comic book venture. We were now soldiers for Christ and would have to be strong enough to withstand many slaps and attacks from the devil. This send-off slap sent us into battle. I liked the "Army of Youth" song and the brave, though militaristic, sentiments expressed in the Confirmation liturgy. I felt that I had missed out on an explicitly spiritual group focus, having gone to a public school. After my father joined the church, my parents decided to send us all to Catholic schools. It was hard to leave the people I knew from the public school, but the thought of attending a Catholic high school that fostered spiritual growth inspired me. I had yet, however, to meet the students who were products of eight years of Catholic education.

Having been both a Brownie and a Girl Scout in the public schools, I had been introduced to the mystique of a uniform. The Catholic high school girls wore navy uniform jackets and skirts, which seemed to give a sense of identity and belonging, as well as carrying an inspiring religious significance. When I started Catholic high school, I found that the girls who wore the uniforms didn't share my enthusiasm, since they had been wearing them for years. Each tried to make her own uniform look unique in some way—the skirt a little shorter, or the Spauldings shoes a little whiter, etc. The sisters spent a great deal of time checking for discrepancies in what appeared to be an ongoing contest. On First Fridays we had "free dress," which encouraged quite a fashion show. Because of the intense heat beginning in the spring and lasting into early fall, our summer uniform consisted of a pastel broadcloth skirt and a white blouse.

One spring the girls started a fad of wearing elaborate mini bouquets at the collar and sporting sunglasses with little flowers on the frames. My sister and I thought of fashioning some enormous flowers out of construction paper and wearing one around each of our eyes, just to get a reaction, but the idea never moved beyond the planning stage. Uniform dress had been intended to foster Christian simplicity and unity, but actually it provided a challenge for adolescent circumvention. As a principal in a high school where I later taught said to the students, "Our job is to enforce the rules; yours is to try to break them."

Another thing I noticed about "Catholic school kids" was a certain over-familiarity with sacred things. One late afternoon I walked into the parish church and saw several little boys in school uniforms running around the sanctuary throwing a kickball between the statues. Did this mean that they felt an easy familiarity in God's house? Hugo Rahner reports in his *Man at Play* that in earlier times there had been a liturgical practice of throwing a ball in church in a playful, celebratory manner.

Somehow I suspected that there was no connection between that early practice and the intentions of the kickball players, in spite of their religious education.

When I was a senior in high school, we had a few days of retreat. We didn't go off the school grounds, but attended talks and read spiritual books. A few girls were quite taken with whatever they were reading, and, even during the time that we were given to walk reflectively outside, took their books and sat outside to read. Later I found out that they had slipped religious-looking book jackets over racy novels, evidently having decided upon a retreat from the retreat.

That year one of my friends who wanted to lose weight put herself on a strict three-banana diet—one for breakfast, one for lunch, one for dinner. On the last day of our retreat, I was walking outside reflecting upon her diet instead of a more spiritual topic. When I tried to turn my mind to religious subjects a thought popped up that made me feel as though I were "going bananas." What if I had a calling to be a nun? I immediately became a bit dizzy and had to lean against one of the wooden posts of the arcade. Thinking about wearing a black and white habit for life was too much for me. Some of the earlier questions I had entertained about sisters came back to me. Did they ever eat? (In those days, sisters always ate privately.) Did they have real feet or wheels? (One of the jokes about sisters when they all wore long habits.) I remembered a parish sodality picnic at a lake. The sisters obviously had feet because they hiked around with us. They had brought a lunch, but went to a table a distance away to eat privately. They must, of course, eat—but what? Hopefully, not something strange. Since my father was a gourmet cook, we were probably spoiled, but then the sisters probably didn't go to the extremes of cooking portions of bear, at least. My thoughts returned to the banana diet—strange in itself. I filed the thought of a religious vocation away for another day.

Near the end of the senior year, I was sitting in the parish school yard on a pleasant, sunny afternoon. When I looked up at the unusually blue sky above the church roof, the cross on the top of the steeple suddenly flashed a brilliant golden light toward me as the sun hit it at just the right angle. I knew it was a sign, a message for further reflection.

The first formal meeting that I remember attending was one held by my senior class just before graduation. I was aware that there were probably as many possibilities to suggest for the graduation plans as there were people in the room. Unfortunately, the few girls who spoke up voiced rather unimaginative ideas, and the outcome was so banal that I wondered why we had spent the time together at all. I concluded that meetings were a waste of time. G. K. Chesterton wrote that, when he was a young child, a grown-up had said to him, "When you grow up you'll change your mind about that." Chesterton reports that the adult's prediction didn't come true. He concluded that changing one's mind on important matters might be the result of mere compromise with conventionality, perhaps a result of jaded aging. I still feel the same way about most meetings.

We graduated in a large auditorium downtown—the same one in which I had resorted to counting the windows during a violin concert when I was ten years old. During the bishop's lengthy graduation homily, I was tempted to recheck the number of windows, but fortunately he sprinkled his speech with references to the name of our school as "St. Hoakim," instead of "San Joaquin," which kept my interest. As we each received our diplomas, we knelt and kissed the bishop's ring. I had always wondered about this practice, but at least it was preferable to kissing the bishop himself.

The next year I began college at Fresno State, majoring in music. My violin teacher, an amiable man, resembled a bear in appearance and movement—a large teddy bear type. An excellent violinist and concertmaster of the college symphony, he was easygoing as a teacher, chewing Juicy Fruit gum and occasionally giving gentle suggestions. In matters other than playing the violin, he didn't seem too practical. When the pencil he was using to mark my music became dull, he attempted to sharpen it on the edge of one of the old heavy wooden doors of the music room. The method wasn't successful. It occurred to me that he was lucky to have a wife to handle matters at home.

My first days on the college campus were confusing; my mind was filled with questions about where to go, what to do, etc. I spied a neatly dressed, confident-looking student, observing things in an aloof, knowing way. "He must be a senior," I thought. After working up the courage to approach him, I asked one of the many questions bothering me, only to find out that he was also a freshman and seemed to know less than I did. A sloppily dressed boy lounging on the ground like a bum was a senior. It was a lesson in facades and might be summed up by the saying: "Always appear confident, especially when you don't know what you're doing."

Changes were in the air whenever a new level of schooling began. I was in the first class to move from the elementary school to the sixth grade at the new junior high school. The high school I attended had only been open for a few years when I started. The college where I took music lessons during my high school years had outgrown its old ivy-covered brick buildings with the heavy doors that were unsuitable as pencil sharpeners. A new campus started farther out from the center of town. While some departments remained on the old campus, others moved to the few buildings completed on the new one, and many of us had classes on both campuses. A common meeting place on the new campus was a Quonset hut that served as a cafeteria in the middle of the open spaces of bare ground. Students of all descriptions from many departments sloshed through the mud in winter and braved the heat in summer to partake of the limited menu, mostly hamburgers.

When I happened to walk to lunch one day with two girls from Japan, one of them said to me, "I feel so sorry for you Catholics. They won't let you eat meat on Fridays." To myself I thought, "You have it wrong. We choose not to eat meat on Friday as a common mortification, following the tradition and directives of the Church." But something about her remark puzzled me. Later the thought came to me: What if some people who don't like meat order lobster on Friday? Is it still a penitential act?

The summer after my freshman year in college, Ellen, a high school classmate of mine who attended USF in San Francisco, found me a job at a restaurant in Yosemite. All the other students working there were from that college. Since I knew only Ellen, and we had different shifts, I initially spent my off hours alone. I worked the night shift from 4:30 p.m. to 1:00 a.m. and sometimes on my nights off walked through the little meadow to our dorms to look up at the stars, shining far above the granite walls. When I first arrived, I spent almost every moment outside looking up at the sheer cliffs, wondering how anyone who lived there could get anything done in the midst of all that grandeur. Once a week, from the top of the cliffs, people from Camp Curry lit a fire, and then pushed the burning embers over the cliff. The visual effect was a waterfall of fire, called the Fire Fall, a startling contrast to the many fascinating waterfalls that fell naturally from the cliffs. It was a wonderfully dramatic sight. One evening, I took my usual walk to see the stars. From Camp Curry on the valley floor someone shouted, "Let the fire fall." Just as the fire fell, a full moon popped up directly above it. The distance must have given the illusion of the moon's speed, but I was awestruck. A number of times that summer, the thought that I might have a religious vocation returned—I felt this was another sign.

When I returned to college in the fall, the feelings of being called to religious life persisted, sometimes distracting me from listening to concerts and recitals. It was an extraordinary idea. What an extreme life choice! Then I remembered a scene from *Mr. Blue*, Miles Connelley's novel about a man who put God before everything else. When someone left him a small fortune, Mr. Blue spent most of it on the poor, using a little to buy colorful cushions and to hire a limousine from which to distribute alms. When he had no money, which was most of the time, he lived in a box on the top of a skyscraper (nearer to God) and flew a red flag with "COURAGE" written on it in bold letters. He seemed to be a model for anyone who followed a daring call.

One day on the way home from school, I decided to stop at the parish rectory, ring the doorbell, and ask a priest if I were imagining things or if God might be prodding me. Synchronistically, there happened to be a vocation director from a religious order staying overnight, so I was delivered into his hands. Using a poker analogy, he told me that I couldn't force God to show His hand. However he added, "If God wants you, He'll get you." I hadn't read the "Hound of Heaven" yet, but later, when I played the violin for a musical version of it written by one of our sisters, I became familiar with the lines and realized that I had experienced a similar hounding myself.

In the spring of my sophomore year, I caught a bad cold. I had picked up a little pamphlet at church about religious vocations and began to read it in my congested condition. The gist of it was that anyone in the world might be called to religious life. It listed objection after objection that people might make in response to the call. It actually appeared to be almost nonsense as I look back on it—even an elephant with a head cold might be called. It was that piece of near nonsense that convinced me that my inner promptings must be valid. Perhaps a case of "nunsense"?

Recovering from the cold, I decided to seek a second opinion and rang the doorbell of the parish convent. The superior/principal talked with me privately in the parlor. She developed an analogy to explain the choice between marriage and religious life. The image was of a street having a sidewalk on either side. The idea was that you could start off on either side and have equal chances of slipping in a puddle near the end. Although this suggestion made about as much sense as the little pamphlet, I felt that I was being called to choose the sidewalk less taken. In my search for clarity, the most illogical arguments made me more confident that I was on the right track. Chesterton's "The Wild Goose Chase," fit the experience in some strange way. He suggests in that short tale that there is nothing in life as fine or holy as a wild goose chase. It leads to places you might not dream of, whether you catch the goose or not.

Following the sister's advice at the end of our talk, I contacted the vocation directress who lived in Los Angeles. She let me know when she would be coming through Fresno, and we set up a meeting. I felt that the cat was out of the bag, and now I was in for it. As soon as we were seated in the parlor, she said primly, "Mona, have you ever thought of becoming a sister?" I thought that either she had missed something or I had. Didn't she remember that I had contacted her as the vocation person? Was it the custom for sisters to pretend that they didn't know what a conversation's purpose is at the beginning—humility, maybe? My question was never answered, but I answered hers, and the process began.

Meanwhile, I had to disclose my plans to my family. My mother said, "I hope it isn't because you haven't been happy here." My sister went immediately into the bathroom and didn't come out for a long time. My father, being a practical man, said, "I think it's a good idea. You tend to drop a few crumbs when eating, and you'll have one of those nice white bibs to catch things." Since he had been converted, he had become an enthusiastic church-goer, the president of the "Young Men's Institute" (most of whom were middle-aged), and an advocate of all things Catholic.

Two

From Novice to Teacher

In the fall of 1956 I was accepted for entrance into the congregation of St. Joseph. The sisters obtained the necessary items I had to take with me. After saying goodbye to everyone, I boarded a plane for Los Angeles, carrying my violin and a *Confidential* magazine that one of my friends wanted me to display for a last minute snapshot. She probably planned to blackmail me with it later—the magazine being thought of as unfit for sisters to hold, much less read. I traveled by myself because an extended car trip with my family would make things harder for all of us. In those days we were not allowed to return home to visit for a number of years. Later I was to read Sister Maris Stella's poem about her entering the convent, entitled "The Veil and the Rock." She wrote, "This was the way that led…a blind going without knowing [but]…. This was the way." The lines could apply to an important choice in anyone's life, but "blind going" seemed particularly fitting, since those of us who entered the convent in the 1950s were told practically nothing about what would happen after we stepped over the threshold.

I wore a dress I really hated, since the clothes worn upon entering were to be kept in a basement downstairs in case a person left the community before vows. In my purse was a partially smoked pack of Salem cigarettes, which looked and smelled like something from a mummy's tomb when I opened the suitcase several years later.

Arriving in the afternoon, we changed shortly afterwards into the black skirt and cape worn by postulants. We were excused from formal prayers that day, but fortunately not from dinner, which that evening was a picnic in the outer yard. It was mid-September and still warm. We stood behind the novices, who were all in full habits, facing a statue in the yard for the grace before meals. At the end of the grace, the black wall of novices turned toward us, and all of them said together, "Good evening, sisters." It was a bit intimidating. Did they think we were sisters already? Maybe we didn't have much of a chance for second thoughts now. I was nervous during the whole dinner, but managed to put away a hot dog.

A year later, when I was one of the habited novices myself, I remembered my own nervousness and was determined to be friendly and compassionate toward any postulant I sat next to at dinner. The young girl I did sit next to was an intrepid type from a large Catholic family and seemed less nervous than I was after having spent a year in the place. Although of a slight, wiry build, she devoured several hot dogs in a row, followed by a big dessert. The next morning she got to work early and scrubbed out a huge stain in a sink in the mop closet. No one had been able to budge that stain before she came. I felt that my intentions had been good, but my compassion might have been better directed elsewhere.

We usually ate our meals in silence, listening to a sister reading from a spiritual work. At breakfast the next morning, the reading was about the saint whose feast fell on that particular day. In addition to keeping silence, we were asked to keep "custody of the eyes," which meant we were not to look around at others. When eating my first silent breakfast, I sneaked a peek at the novice across from me. She held her eyelids down so deliberately that I wondered if she could see her plate. I continued to take occasional peeks, but no change. I hoped that she was all right, and also that I would be allowed a little more leeway, so as to be able to see my food. I couldn't get a glimpse of her eyes that morning, but I was destined to look into them frequently several years later. She turned out to be a primary teacher at the first school where I was sent to teach. Her eyes were big, brown and expressive. She was put in charge of me, a fledgling teacher. I remember her eyes welling up with tears one day when I confessed to her that I hadn't followed the plans in the teacher's guide for a particular lesson.

The daily schedule in the novitiate began with a thirty-minute meditation in the morning, followed by Mass. We were encouraged to arrive in the chapel as soon as possible after rising to the sound of the five o'clock bell, so as to spend a few moments of private prayer before the common prayer began. Although I think the underlying purpose of this practice was to be sure everyone arrived on time for common prayer, some took on the early arrival time as an athletic challenge. A contest developed to see who could dress the fastest and be the first one there. Individuality dictated various methods of achieving speed. We were not allowed to sleep in our clothes, but we slept in alcoves around which we could draw curtains. Some people must have developed a fireman's skill of setting up their wardrobe, such as it was, for maximum performance. One girl admitted at the recreation period, when we were allowed to talk, that she had skipped brushing her teeth. It made for top speed, she said, and "The Lord doesn't mind." She might have been better versed in incarnational theology. We sat in designated places, and after that revelation I was glad not to have to sit next to her.

An actual athletic contest took place in October when we postulants had a recreation day with the novices. Altogether, we numbered almost two hundred. Those who played volleyball formed themselves into a postulant team versus a novice team. The day was a sort of mini-fair and picnic. I joined two other postulants who played the violin and entertained in a "fiddlers' corner."

The novices won the game. Afterward, I walked into the building next to a novice and remarked, "Your team played very well." She said, "I wasn't on it." I found her answer disconcerting, but also refreshing in the midst of so much collectivity. Whereas most girls who entered religious life at that time came directly from high school, she had obtained a college degree and had traveled and studied in Europe before entrance. Her remark reflected the broader view she had gained through education and experience.

Ordinarily our schedules as postulants didn't vary, but one day a visiting priest arrived to say an extra Mass at ten o'clock in the morning. The sister in charge of us, called the "postulant mistress," made an announcement after breakfast, saying, "You may go to the second Mass this morning." Thinking that, although the Mass was sacred and inspiring, one was sufficient for the day, I wandered down the hall near our common room, enjoying the free morning minutes. After very few, I was apprehended in the hall by the postulant mistress. She was much taller than I, and in full habit. I wasn't used to encountering her alone, especially in a dark hallway. She said meaningfully, "I said that you may go to the second Mass." "May" obviously meant one thing to her and another to me. A few years later, when I was in the novitiate, the novice mistress, who had been on her yearly retreat, told us that she had been to a large retreat house and had been able to attend ten Masses in one day. I was astounded. Why would ten be better than one? The American ideal of quantity as being better than quality seemed to have invaded even the spiritual realm.

During the thirty-minute meditation periods, one in the early morning before Mass and one as part of the five o'clock afternoon prayer, we were supposed to reflect on a scriptural verse or a scene from the gospels. I had trouble imaginatively placing myself in a scene from the gospels, such as the Sermon on the Mount. In trying to picture the scene, I kept wondering exactly what the disciples' sandals looked like or how long their beards were. For me it was more an exercise in uninformed imagination than a prayer. Once we were allowed to go outside for a meditation period. I sat on a little hill of grass, which now must be underneath the impressive chapel that was later built on that site, looked at the bright green grass in the sunlight and thought, "What now?" Many years later, I heard the story about the monk who entered a

Zen monastery and said to another who had been there for a while, "What's next?" The older monk answered, "Nothing's next—This is it." It wasn't too bad—just mysterious.

In November it appeared that there really wouldn't be anything next. I was getting used to the regular schedule. Winter didn't seem to make any significant changes in the Los Angeles area. In Fresno we didn't have snow, but the air turned colder, sometimes frost developed, and the leaves turned beautiful colors. But even without a change to colder weather, I felt much like Ishmael does at the beginning of *Moby Dick*. "Whenever I find myself growing grim about the mouth; whenever it is damp, drizzly November in my soul;…then, I account it high time to get to sea as soon as I can." I was ready for an adventure, but I saw no ship on the horizon. It was dark by afternoon prayer at that time of year.

One of those evenings after prayers, we went to the dining room as usual, expecting one of the regular fares. What a surprise—the place had been turned into a party room! A special dinner was served, followed by petit fours for dessert—something I'd never had before. After dinner, we climbed the hill to the college and were treated to a play about St. Stanislaus, a patron of young religious, whose feast we celebrated that day. The novices played all the parts, including that of a crusty old professor who had influenced the young saint. It was a top-notch surprise party—the surprise probably the more easily kept, since the novices and postulants didn't mix often, and there was a rule of silence for most of each day. The tradition was to keep it a secret from the group entering the next year. It was a great idea and had been planned to be given just when we needed it.

After the excitement of St. Stanislaus Day, November 13, the schedule returned to normal for a few weeks. Then the Advent season began, in preparation for Christmas. The readings and music were beautiful, particularly the chanting of the "O Antiphons," a novena sung nine days before Christmas. Each day a different title for Christ was used: "O Wisdom," "O Root of Jesse," "O Key of David," "O Rising Day Star," etc.

Advent was an even more silent, prayerful time than that of the ordinary daily routine. It proved quite a challenge for me and began to seem endless. When Christmas arrived, the contrast was almost too startling in the common room—every inch was decorated. Candy canes abounded, as did loads of festoons and other sweets, but there were no familiar family faces, no gift exchanges between near and dear ones.

After the holidays we all took a semester of religion, focusing on Catholic doctrine. Because I had not attended a Catholic grammar school, I had learned nowhere near the number of catechism answers that most of the others knew by heart. Therefore, I failed the comprehensive catechism test and was placed in what seemed to be a "dumbbell" religion class. I felt a little chagrined, since I had been reading Thomas à Kempis, Fulton Sheen and *America* magazine during my two years in college. But one had to know the memorized answers. Actually, the few of us who landed in the class rather enjoyed it. Evidently the sister in charge realized that we wouldn't be able to memorize in a semester the amount of material covered during eight years of Catholic grammar school. So we engaged in varied types of learning. At the end of the course we gave a little skit for the more educated ones in the upper class. It was based on the gospel story of the rich man, Dives, who lived well and never shared anything with Lazarus, the poor beggar at his gate. The rich man was subsequently thrown into the flames of hell, and the poor man was taken to Abraham's Bosom—somewhere near heaven. Before he died, the best Lazarus could hope for was that the dogs would wander up to him and lick his sores. I played the part of Lazarus, bandaged from head to toe and sitting in a wheelchair. The hit of the show was the convent dog that walked on stage and licked the piece of chocolate placed between my toes. I had probably gotten more out of reading *America* magazine, but the skit was fun.

The postulancy lasted six months. At the end of that time, those who were accepted into the novitiate received and donned the religious habit at a Reception ceremony. In the preceding months, however, we had to make our own habits from pieces of black serge. I had never been proficient at sewing, but I managed to finish mine in time. Two others almost missed the deadline. During recreation period the evening before the deadline, we all gathered around in the common room to watch a team of competent seamstresses hover over each of the unfinished habits, which were laid out in the middle of the floor. It was like watching two teams of paramedics. Getting into the spirit of the thing, we all cheered them on, as if they were competing in a small athletic arena. Black thread went whizzing through the unfinished sleeves and pleats. But we didn't take sides. In fact, the last one finished received a bigger ovation than the first.

Somewhere along the line—it must have been a long while back—someone had decided that all sisters in habits should wear corsets to improve their posture, etc. This was one item we didn't have to make for ourselves, fortunately. Although we had some vague notion that corsets were part of the official garb, I don't remember having been told directly. In the days before the chapel was built, we used a set of consecutive classrooms for prayer. The inner walls were folding doors that, when open, could make the three rooms into one to accommodate a large group. One afternoon all of us—postulants, novices, professed sisters—were at the afternoon meditation. Perhaps a few of us were "resting with God" in a brief, prayerful doze, sitting upright. The chapel windows looked out over a laundry yard, which extended into the large asphalt area used for recreation, parking and delivery trucks. Suddenly a man shouted, "MAY COMPANY!" from beneath the windows. Everyone returned to ground zero and the novices behind us began to giggle. Evidently the deliveryman, having tried the front doorbell and a knock on the side door, had resorted to lung power to get a response. Some of us didn't realize until later that our corsets had arrived.

My previous corset experience was limited to having observed the one worn by my grandmother who lived with us. Her name was Helen, which became "Nell" to her friends. She referred to her corset as her

"Little Nellie Cover." The term had puzzled me as a child, since the cover couldn't be seen from the outside and, although my grandmother was small for a woman, she didn't seem little to me. I did see her corset a few times when she laundered it. It looked to me like some sort of military armor for Victorian women. Little did I know that I would wear a contraption like that someday myself. In the years following the noviate, I heard a number of corset stories, one from a sister who taught in grammar school. The corsets were pink with white narrow stays in them that sometimes didn't. Unfortunately, one of her stays decided to leave as the sister walked between the children's desks. A little boy helpfully picked it up and called out, "Sister, you dropped your ruler!"

Shortly before the Reception Day, on which we received the habit, we all went on a hike up the fire road in the hills behind the college. We stopped quite a way up the trail and had a picnic. Far beyond any sign of a residential district, we sat on the ground where there was some natural vegetation. Later we found out that part of it was poison oak. As a result, two novices had rashes on their faces and had to eat in a private dining room. I discovered a rash all over my legs. A sister nurse met me at 4:30 in the morning each day thereafter to cover both my legs with ointment and gauze, which reminded me of my Lazarus costume. The procedure had to be done before I put on the long black stockings required. Unfortunately, the condition lasted through the Reception Day itself.

In those days, we wore long bridal dresses and veils to the first part of the ceremony; then we left the chapel to be habited and returned having been transformed into novices, wearing the full habit for the rest of the ceremony. I had the distinction of having my legs covered with gauze before putting on what I then thought of as my last pair of see-through nylon stockings. Thank goodness the dresses were long! Although we were "brides of Christ," not destined to become mommies, I now looked like a "mummy" underneath the gown. When we left the ceremony in order to put on the habit, we were each assigned a couple of experienced sisters to dress us properly. The bridal gowns were all different, selected through personal choice, but the habits made us look so similar that one of the sisters who dressed me didn't recognize me when I walked by her on my way back from the ceremony.

After becoming novices, we moved from our postulant common room to the much larger novitiate room. We first-year novices shared it with those who were now second-year novices. Our novice mistress was German—tough but fair. She told us that our feelings didn't count and introduced us to one of the main dictums of religious life: "Keep the Rule, and the Rule will keep you." In addition to the rule of silence and prayer, we were given a set of lesser obligations referred to as "Points of Obedience." These directives included such things as how often to polish one's shoes and how many glasses of water to drink daily. Although I never developed a serious respect for these points, I did respect her. She obviously had our welfare in mind and demonstrated her concern admirably one night at dinner. The custom was to line up in our designated places, referred to as "rank," and to stand behind our chairs until grace before meals was finished. On this particular evening our novice mistress spotted a mouse near the curtains of the dining room. She whipped off one of her sturdy shoes in an instant, and went after it. I can't remember whether she hit it or not, but was impressed by her quick, positive action.

Having had a musical background, I was most appreciative of the beauty of the Gregorian Chant that we sang often for Mass and prayer. I hadn't known there was such an extensive wealth of chant for all the liturgical seasons and feast days. I wished that more chant had been used in ordinary parish liturgies, and felt that much of the church was missing out on this, the most beautiful church music, as it seemed to me.

When I was a second-year novice John XXIII became pope. It was a major international event; Pius XII had been pope since I was three years old. We hadn't read newspapers or listened to the radio since we entered, but we were allowed to listen to a broadcast of the election in Rome. I wasn't sure that I understood any of it, but I knew it signaled a major change. In fact, no one could have imagined the extent of the changes that would result from the meeting of the Second Vatican Council that Pope John assembled.

I had noticed gradual changes in minor practices and customs since I had become a novice. As in my school days, I was in on the beginning of something new. I had heard that shortly before I entered, it was the custom to spring out of bed at the sound of the morning bell and kiss the floor as a gesture of prayerful humility. I was thankful this custom had been dropped, even though we cleaned the building so thoroughly and so often that it wouldn't have been dangerous to our health. I wrote a short poem about the routine cleaning, when it had begun to feel a little too regular to me.

The Building
Always clean
Never give the dust a chance to fall
Always rectangular
Squares on the ceiling and on the wall
Always the same
People come and people go
And people the building.

During the first year of the novitiate, we took whatever classes we needed at the college, but the second year was deemed a canonical year and was restricted to religious studies only. Although most girls who entered at that time had only finished a high school education, I and a few others of my group had attended some college courses prior to entering. Since we had credits for the equivalent of one of the courses the others were taking, a special class was held for six of us, entitled "Christian Archeology." Our professor was an elderly sister whose veil occasionally fell down over her face during her lectures. We attended the class in one of the classrooms adjacent to the temporary chapel. After class, the folding doors were opened to allow more room for a prayer of examination of conscience that everyone attended just before lunch. Then the six of us went out down the hallway and back into the front of the first classroom, which was closest to the altar. All the others had taken their places in the chapel early, but we were released only a minute or two before the prayer, so as to complete the time needed for class. We were highly visible as we filed in before everyone's eyes.

One day during class some of us must have been suffering from "routine fatigue." Our instructor began describing the sufferings that the early martyrs of the church had endured. Her description of their having been tied onto blocks of ice and frozen to death was one of the most graphic saints' stories I had ever heard. It was punctuated with several inadvertent slips of sister's veil down over her eyes. She adroitly flipped the veil back each time, as if brushing away flies. We did our utmost to suppress giggles, but at least one telltale sound erupted. The professor, although seated, seemed to rise up above us in indignation. "You laugh at the torments of the martyrs!?!" We then suffered a few tormenting moments ourselves until the end of class. Released from the class at last, we stumbled into the chapel, still fighting for control, but unable to suppress a few snorts and giggles. From that day until the end of the semester, the other novices eagerly awaited our entrance, in case we disgraced ourselves again. It wasn't that they weren't prayerful, but any variation in the routine was welcome at that stage of our training.

I recall a recreation period when a number of us were sharing stories of how we had been called to religious life. One of our group was a former marine, who had entered about the same time as I had. Walking away from the group, she shared her story with me. As a marine she had of necessity spent hours standing at attention on the parade ground. She told me that having had so many hours to reflect upon the deep truths of life, she had decided that the most important thing in the world was a good steak and a glass of wine. We became friends instantly. After so many in-depth and dramatic accounts, her humor exemplified Oscar Wilde's remark: "Life is too important be taken seriously."

In order to encourage a humble anonymity, the novitiate superiors did not allow us to speak much about our personal families nor to draw attention to ourselves as individuals. However, when I found out the birthday of one the novices in our group, I left a message on a piece of paper in which I had rolled up a small token. Someone must have found out about it and reported it because the novice mistress spent most of the weekly conference (a lecture to instill in us proper religious practices) on the subject of the inappropriate nature of personal gifts. My twenty-first birthday followed shortly thereafter. I spent a number of hours that day off the road and down the hillside with other novices scaling fish that a benefactor had donated. I'm sure it was a unique activity for someone living in my century on one's twenty-first birthday. (Quite a fishy way to celebrate a landmark.)

At the end of the two-year novitiate, a group of superiors met to decide which of us would be approved to make temporary vows. The day of the meeting was a laundry day. Once a week we all shared in the job, being assigned to specific tasks, such as running a large mangle in the laundry room to press the linens, etc. Some novices starched those parts of the habit that needed it, others hung out underwear on the line. Occasionally, people who had already done their assigned work were called down later when the ironing had piled up in greater amounts than the usual crew could handle. In the afternoon I was sitting in the novitiate common room, reflecting on my situation. If "they" sent me home now, it seemed almost a matter of indifference to me. I felt that I had done what I could and it was now up to God. When the call came asking for extra help in the laundry near five o'clock, I decided not to go. I had always responded to the call, but was a little tired. Besides, I thought that if all the important people who might be observing us were at the meeting, my fate was sealed already, and making a good impression might be the only reason (and a bad one at that) for going down to help.

Soon after that day, we were told that all of our group had been accepted to make vows. The traditional day for the ceremony was on March 19, the feast day of St. Joseph. We each carried a lighted candle in procession into the large chapel that had recently been completed. The sanctuary and altar were of marble. Angels adorned the chandeliers; stained glass windows, backed in red and blue, displayed symbols from the litany of St. Joseph. I was quite aware of the gravity of the moment, and so was my candle. It kept shivering as if it were a wand that had discovered deep water and wanted to jump out of my hand. Was this really happening? How presumptuous, I felt, to actually be professing to become one of what some people called "the good sisters." Had all the good sisters once been just girls with shaking candles answering an unfathomable call? In any case, the chanting of the lovely "Veni Creator" and the fragrant scent of Easter lilies banking the altar combined to form what is now a hauntingly beautiful memory.

At the ceremony we each received our profession crucifix, which hung on a cord around the neck and appeared below the white cape or gimp that my father had considered to be a potential bib. The next day we resumed our regular schedule, which always included taking turns waiting on table. At many meals in the winter we had soup, which the servers carried in large round tureens, hot from the kitchen. After making vows, some of us forgot that we were wearing a fairly large metal crucifix and frequently hit it against the pew when kneeling, etc. I remember an enthusiastic sister of my group, feeling rather elated by her new status as a professed sister. She smiled broadly as she gladly carried the large soup tureen toward our table. I tried not to look, but couldn't help seeing her shiny new cross dangling in the soup. It was one of the meals in silence, so I didn't mention it, and it didn't seem to have affected the soup at all.

Meanwhile, the pattern of change, which had begun when I entered, continued. A large chapel and a Juniorate building were completed by the time I made first vows. The Juniorate period was also new. Formerly, sisters had been sent out directly after vows to schools or hospitals.

Usually those assigned to be teachers completed their education on Saturdays and in summer school, while already teaching full time. Some of us called it "Learn while you teach" (a saying that I found to be true for all teachers, no matter how well educated).

The Juniorate was a two-year program, providing time for college classes. For me it was an enriching period because I enjoyed study, and was able to roam the library and explore the worlds of poetry, philosophy, theology, and good fiction. Much of what I found valuable I discovered on my own, outside of assigned classes. Many of my group didn't share my enthusiasm and would have preferred to have begun a more active life right away. But there were periods in the day when we all felt we might like to have a little more excitement. A bit of physical exercise broke the routine when we were called upon to do some cleaning at the college during the girls' vacations. I was assigned to the biology lab once, and came across a package of radish seeds that someone had thrown into the wastebasket. I took them back down the hill to the House of Studies where we lived. There my regular assignment, or "charge," was to clean some of the rooms in the large parlor area, all of which had a number of potted plants. In order to make the daily work more interesting, I planted a radish seed in each of the pots. Having obtained a little notebook for quotations and observations, I recorded the progress of one of the seeds that I had planted in a special pot belonging to the Provincial Superior placed in front of the Sacred Heart statue near the entrance:

July 13, 1959: A radish is growing in Sr. Josephine's potted plant. It only took three days.

July 16, 1959: Sr. Josephine's radish leaf is very long.

July 20, 1959: Great sadness has befallen the earth—the radish in Sr. Josephine's pot was uprooted. (Someone else must have been checking on the special pot.)

Although I was majoring in music, I spent a good deal of time reading poetry. I had always been a reader, but mainly of prose, with some nonsense poetry for variety, including the humorous verse found in Walt Kelly's "Pogo." I checked out anthologies of poetry and jotted down favorite lines in my notebook, sprinkled between radish reports, personal observations, and important lines from other works. It was a secret project, following the Pogo dictum: "Anybody can pretend to be smart—it takes the real McCoy to pass yourself off as an idiot." I included the notes on my musical education also, such as recording the information that a composer named Marais had written a keyboard piece called, "The Gall Bladder Operation."

Eventually I tried a few lines of poetry myself. Walking down the hill after class on a winter afternoon at dusk, I saw Los Angeles lying below me through a light layer of fog:

At dusk
The city lies in mists of pink and blue;
Small sparks from the machinery
Peek through.

Looking down from our hill on the morning of a recollection (retreat) day the same winter I was delighted by a colorful bird that flew up out of the bushes. I waited to see it again, but it didn't return. Just as I was about to turn away, it surprised me. How mysteriously free wild things are, I thought. They can't be forced to appear by any degree of wishing—only waiting. I jotted down another haiku:

The fog
Is twisted 'round
The stumps and clumps of hills
All dark, until the bush lets fly—
Red wings.

When spring came, acacias growing near the pathway down from the college bloomed magically overnight. The green branches had been there all winter, but I hadn't paid much attention to them—they were quite spectacular in bloom and conjured up another verse:

I dreamed
A dream of trees
Whose yellow boughs o'er hang
The stairs of every year, unseen
'Til spring.

Christmas vacation from the college began during Advent. We spent many hours cleaning the building we lived in, maintaining enough quiet for reflection. In the postulancy, the somewhat empty time during November had felt a bit too quiet, relieved only by the St. Stanislaus party. In the novitiate, I had taken a part in the evening's play myself, playing the part of Stanislaus' crusty old professor. A few days before the play I had four wisdom teeth pulled at the same time. My face was quite swollen when I went on stage, so I felt that I probably resembled the old gentleman more closely than I ordinarily would have. Although all of my wisdom had been taken from me at once, I could still play the part of the respected mentor.

Whereas the quiet of Advent was a challenge to endure in my first few years, in the Juniorate it passed too quickly. I had grown to appreciate the reflective time. The custom of rising at 5:00 a.m. and going directly to the chapel for meditation followed by Mass had seemed unnatural to me as a postulant, but I valued the stillness of the morning as a Juniorate sister. I tried to capture the atmosphere of the morning Mass in a poem:

Strategy
Here at dark of dawn
We meet in secret
To hold God's last city,
Recapture lost, forgotten dreams,
As Bethlehem descends to Calvary again.

Here the unseen light
Holds court and plans
A subtle web of invasions,
A scheme of tender maneuvers directed
Toward capturing the universe

Here is slight movement
And no sound save that
Of a tiny alarm of a bell
Unheard outside these walls by those
Who have no ears to hear.

That Christmas vacation I checked out a book that one of the English classes was reading. Because I had met the English requirements before I had entered, most of my classes were in music. The book I procured was C. S. Lewis' *Out of the Silent Planet*. The sister librarian who stamped the book for me said, "Have you never read this?" I hadn't, I admitted. She added, "You have a treat in store for you." She was right. One of my favorite places was a rooftop area over the Juniorate building. I carried the book up there, and began an adventure with Ransom, the hero. We took off in a space ship, leaving the silent planet (Earth) behind. We landed on Malacandra (Mars) and found an ancient unfallen world of natural beauty. There we learned that the Bent One had invaded the Earth to such an extent, that communication between Earth and the other planets had been severed for centuries. Ransom eventually met the guiding Spirit of Malacandra, who told him, "You are guilty of no evil…except a little fearfulness…the journey you go on is your pain, and perhaps your cure: For you must be either mad or brave before it is ended." The Spirit (Oyarsa) commissioned Ransom to watch out for the bent ones who would perpetrate evil on the Earth, when he returned. It wasn't long before I joined Ransom for the adventures in the other two books of the trilogy. In *Perelandra* (Venus) Ransom joins in a fight to save its pure inhabitants from a Fall into sin. Back on Earth, he battles scientists ruled by the Bent One in *That Hideous Strength*.

In January the quiet vacation ended. The crèche remained up in the chapel until the official end of the liturgical season of Christmas. Gazing on the peaceful Bethlehem scene, I realized that Lent would begin within the next month. The irony I felt expressed itself in another poem:

Aftermath
The crib glows red
Against the chapel wall.
Even now we hear
Soldiers shuffling feet,
See lanterns and clubs.
"Where is He
Born King of the Jews?
We have seen his star in the West
And are come to crucify Him."

We had a recreation hour after lunch on the Juniorate schedule during which our superior liked to play cards in the community room. A number of our group joined her, but I preferred to take a walk outside around the hill, since activities were optional. The superior gradually formed the idea that I might be secretly "against the government" for some reason. She indicated her suspicions in one of our private talks. I had just finished a philosophy class and explained my point of view, referring to the difference I had learned between a practical and a speculative judgment. She didn't appear to have taken the class and just sent me off to the chapel to "consider"—meaning to pray and reflect about my judgment in general, I suppose.

After that talk, whenever she went away for a few days, she admonished me in a friendly, almost teasing manner, saying, "Behave yourself, while I'm gone." I resisted her influence for a while by continuing to choose walking over group card games, but when she brought up the issue specifically, I realized that she would feel better if I joined the card players. We only had a few weeks left in the first year of the Juniorate. I went in to one of the shower rooms, closed the door, and sat on the small ledge, considering my position. After weighing the alternatives, I decided I'd better play cards—she held all the important cards that would decide my future.

Those last few weeks dragged. We rarely left the hill, except for doctors' appointments. The afternoons were particularly long. However, during the extended periods of study in my room, I began to notice a cheery flock of birds singing in the late afternoon and into the twilight. I imagined that they shared my restlessness. Later in the year they disappeared, so I remembered them in a sonnet:

The Night Birds
Although I know that they are gone from here,
I sometimes hear them calling, calling still,
That flock of birds that sang upon the hill
At dusk, to ward away night's soon approaching fear.
I do not know the cause for which they sang
Such lively songs when day was nearly gone.
They should, it seems, have sung those songs at dawn,
For morning shade does not stay long to hang
A shadow on the air. And yet perhaps

In wisdom born to all wild things that thrive
In rock or bush through seasons damp and dry,
They felt a restlessness as dusk, that wraps
The hills in softest gray, began to drive
Their songs away with softer cricket cries.

The next year some of us were sent out to teach, while others remained to continue studies. Those of us who began teaching lived at the school convents during the week and returned to the Juniorate on weekends. I was assigned a second and third grade combination class. Both boys and girls comprised the third grade, but only two rows of little girls, the second. Having no credential and no practice teaching experience, I met daily with the principal for direction. The children were lively and cute—particularly the second grade girls. I began to realize that they should be talked to like people, not infants. One day a representative from the telephone company came to talk to the class. She talked down to them, almost as if she were addressing babies. Some of them asked me later if there was something wrong with her.

Although we got along rather well, a few of the second graders were uncertain about my identity. In those days we all wore standard black walking shoes. In a confidential moment on the playground, one of the second graders, sent as a representative, asked me whether I was a man or a woman—the shoes looked like men's to them, and the long habit didn't reveal much. I told them the truth, but some were skeptical, probably because I joked with them frequently. In fact, I had overheard my nickname for that year, "Mony Baloney," whispered between two of them. All teachers have nicknames, but student security is such that they may teach for many years happily uninformed of their own colorful pseudonyms.

The second grade representative sent to check out my gender was a charming cutie with big brown eyes. Years later, I regretfully heard that she became rather spoiled, but perhaps it was inevitable. I tried my hand at a poem about her:

To Mary, Age 7

In your eyes
Are brown butterflies
Eyelash wings tremble in the breeze.
Stay gently,
Then dart into the sun
For you are one
With the butterflies.

The next year I taught the fifth grade. That year we didn't return to the hill on the weekends, except for Saturday classes. I missed the time on the weekends to walk the fire road that wandered into undisturbed nature areas and to pour through the library, taking newfound treasures back to read on the rooftop. However, by spending the weekend in the school convent, I came to know some of the sisters who lived with me a little better. A music education program on the radio called "The Standard Hour" became part of the curriculum and was played over the P.A. into our classrooms each week. The writers of the program, perhaps anticipating multicultural trends (or trying to combine geography and sociology with music appreciation in one hour) drifted away from presenting truly standard works. Soon it was commonplace for us to be listening to simulated safari trips into dense jungles to hear flutes made out of dry reeds produce one or two repeated notes.

Another sister and I created a parody of the "Standard Hour" and recorded it on tape. We used the sisters teaching in the school for examples of local color. The principal was teaching the eighth grade about the Second World War. From her classroom, our listeners could hear sounds of marching music and shouts of "Heil, Hitler" as if addressed to the teacher. The sister with large brown eyes, whom I had observed at breakfast some years ago, now taught the first grade. Many times she didn't stop teaching when she stepped out into the corridor to close her door. We recorded her usual words: "And one kitty cat and two kitty cats are—SLAM." One empathetic sister who taught seventh grade was heard outside of her classroom sympathizing with a crying girl. Not having mastered all the vocabulary words she taught, she was saying, "Oh, I feel so buxom for you." One segment was based on an incident that had occurred in my classroom after I had encouraged a boy to bring a large pet bird to school. It had flown up to the top of the venetian blinds and I was heard saying, "Whose bright idea was this, anyway?" We used direct quotations from the original incidents, but changed the names to protect the guilty.

At summer school that year, I had to take education classes. I was deeply interested in learning more about truth, beauty, and human development, but these classes didn't seem to fit the bill. Subsequently, I received the only two "D's" of my life in "education" classes. One was a math education class. I found it boring and spent some of the class time pondering information I had gleaned from a sister taking a higher math class:

> Hooray for a ray to infinity
> We view it with great equanimity.
> But to consider a ray
> Would take us all day
> And we wouldn't have time for our dinnerty.

I also took an audiovisual class. Although I later became quite adept at using AV materials, being known as "Movie Mona" one year when I thoroughly explored the film resources in the local library, the theory aspect didn't hold my attention. I made the mistake of turning in a project a week ahead, using big pictures and brief captions—I thought this approach would appeal to the teacher. I needed more free time to finish reading *War and Peace*, an extracurricular project of mine. However, the teacher was not pleased. She evidently required many long pages of parroted jargon. She returned it to me for a second chance, but I was too involved in the human development of Pierre in Tolstoy's novel. Anyway, I failed to see what reams of uninteresting writing had to do with anything, either audio or visual.

Near the end of the summer, all the sisters studying at the college gathered in a large room on July 26, St. Anne's Day, to receive assignments for the next year, as was our custom. The assignments were referred to as "missions" and were read aloud from a podium by one of the sister superiors present. We always packed our trunks at the end of each school year to be prepared for a possible new mission. We sat awaiting our fate as our names and missions were called one by one. That year I was changed from the school in Los Angeles to another parish grammar school in the San Fernando Valley.

In September I taught a fourth grade class. They were a responsive group, but as the year wore on, and I became more familiar with the routine of the curriculum, it became rather tedious. I felt as though I were under water blowing bubbles of simplified information to lively, colorful fish. I continued searching the library for enlightenment and discovered C. S. Lewis' *Chronicles of Narnia*. In the Juniorate, when reading Lewis's works intended for adults, I had looked at one of the Narnia books, and decided it was too juvenile to bother with. I later discovered that during adolescence and sometimes early adulthood, one is too "old" to appreciate the simplicity of fairy tale genre. Lewis himself reveals this truth to Lucy, his godchild, to whom the first book is dedicated. "I wrote this story for you, but when I began it I had not realized that girls grow quicker than books. As a result you are already too old for fairy tales,…but someday you will be old enough to start reading fairy tales again."

The fourth grade reading period had become less interesting as the year went on, perhaps because of the type of stories in their readers. I varied the practice of their reading aloud individually by bringing in a small stepladder and allowing the chosen reader to climb as far up as he or she desired when reading. Soon they were volunteering readily. Finally I decided to read to them from the Narnia tales that I was enjoying, and the reading interest picked up considerably. The class began to take out other volumes from the nearby library. A few months later, a visiting local librarian told me that all of the C. S. Lewis Narnia books had been consistently checked out from her library recently and she was considering ordering second copies. I had read extensively in Lewis' writings by that time and felt that I would like to write him a letter to thank him for his wonderful spiritual insights and delightful fiction. Unfortunately, I procrastinated and found out later that he had died during the year that my fourth graders and I had been enjoying him so much—on November 22, 1963.

Three

Many Changes

Although I didn't hear about Lewis's death until later, my fourth grade class and I heard shocking news over the P.A. that same day, November 22, shortly before lunch. Upon reflection, I thought it rather strange to communicate such a violent act directly to children, but the administration must have been thinking of the historical importance of the assassination, if anyone was thinking clearly that day. Filtered through static, we heard the report of the attack on President John F. Kennedy broadcast live from Dallas.

One of the sisters I lived with was a seasoned teacher who was extremely conservative in her political views—an advocate of the John Birch Society. Returning to the convent for lunch, I met her in the kitchen where she exclaimed, "God has saved the nation!" The assassin's name had not been revealed to the public yet, but she evidently thought the shot had come straight from heaven. (The fact that there was more than one shot didn't seem to bother her. Could God miss?)

The next day, another sister and I drove over the pass into Los Angeles to visit our hospital there. A few cars were on the highway, moving along as if nothing had happened. The contrast between the tragedy and the bright morning, with life going on as usual, reminded me of the way I had felt when I first experienced the death of a person I had known when I was a freshman in high school.

Our English teacher had assigned us a composition about one thing we really liked. A classmate chosen to read hers aloud revealed that she loved to buy high heels in different colors to match different outfits. Shortly afterwards, she contracted polio and was placed in an iron lung, where she died. The morning after her death was sunny and beautiful. I wondered how that could be—surely the world must be changed by her death. I hadn't known her very well and didn't join the group of girls at the funeral who hadn't known her any better, but carried on with loud sobs as if they had cared deeply for her. Their behavior and the beauty of the day after her death were equally mysterious to me.

However, that twenty-third of November, there were not as many cars on the road as usual. Since it was a Saturday, many people were probably at home watching news about the assassination investigation. When we arrived at the hospital, the Irish superior, who knew the political sentiments of our John Bircher, took us aside and whispered, "Have they fingerprinted her yet?" It was a little dark for American humor, but ridiculous enough to lighten our spirits a bit.

I had admired J.F.K. as being an idealist and a supporter of the arts and cultural pursuits in general. People eulogized him as having been a modern day Arthur, trying to establish a graceful democracy for "one brief shining moment," etc. He certainly spoke in an inspiring manner. I wrote a sonnet, attempting to juxtapose the violence of his death with the ideals I thought he stood for. Although the season at the time of the assassination was late autumn, I felt that Kennedy had been cut down in the springtime of his efforts to build a better world.

The Assyrians
We saw them there upon the distant hill
A flock of lambs half-hidden in spring mist.
A most ungainly group it was, and still
The certain dignity which we insist
Was theirs as they walked warm into the sun

Caught us off guard as if a ray of light
From some lone comet hurled from space had won
A small but brilliant battle with the night.
We turned north then—it was the last we saw
Of lambs or peaceful fields just turning green.
Our stubbled lands were still but for the caw
Of crows above the ashen battle scenes.
Always the hollow clank of armor sings
A contrapuntal dissonance with spring.

Our trip into Los Angeles was not unusual, in that those of us who hadn't finished our degrees drove over the pass on the old Sepulveda Road to attend college classes every Saturday. Another sister and I were the youngest in the group and usually rode backwards in the rear of the convent station wagon. The road was full of curves that were prohibitive of our indulging in a hearty breakfast before leaving. It wasn't a natural way to travel, but it did match the analogy suggested by an ancient philosopher who stated that our lives resemble the visual experience of a person rowing a boat. The rower, seated backwards, can only see what is to the right and to the left on the riverbank, in addition to the receding landscape, but can never see what is ahead.

The analogy not only fit the station wagon ride, but in retrospect fit our unawareness of the extent of the upcoming changes in the church and religious life. Church practices at that time were crystal clear, and based on age-old traditions. The Mass was still said in Latin. Our pastor had mastered the ritual to such an extent that he probably said the shortest Mass in Southern California. He had a habit of rubbing his thumbs and index fingers together in tiny circular motions as he spieled off the Latin. He gave the illusion of having tiny phonograph records on his thumbs that played faster than the normal speed, producing a chattering sound like the children's chipmunk record. Perhaps it was chipmunk Latin. I sometimes wondered how he adapted a few years later, when the English Mass was introduced.

Although I eventually taught all the other grades in elementary school, I was never assigned a first grade class. It was probably just as well, because I had a tendency to play with first graders. On yard duty I sometimes played "witch" with them, swirling my black habit about and saying "I'll get you, my pretties." We all enjoyed the game, but I no doubt compromised my responsibilities in the yard. I hate to think what might have happened in the classroom had I been their teacher.

That summer I had to take a class in the "new math." It wasn't any more appealing to me than the old math. The method attempted to enlighten the students about the make up of mathematical concepts by the use of visual aids. When I read the directions in one of the new teaching manuals for a lesson on the decimal system, I was certain the author had never been in the classroom. It read, "Hold up ten candies in front of the children." I could imagine a stampede toward the front of the room occurring, and perhaps bodily harm coming to the teacher, since there were always at least thirty children per class. (No doubt my fantasy either underestimated the children's manners, or overestimated their boldness.)

My troubles with math had begun in my own grammar school years and continued into junior high school. The struggle to solve "thought problems" turned the math period into an endless purgatory. The problems sounded like stories, but were too predictable to bother reading or figuring out—predictable in the sense that they ended with a number (which number it was didn't interest me). A trip to the restroom to break the monotony became more exciting.

My interests definitely lay more with imaginative, figurative thought. Years later I proved to be a dominant intuitive on the Myers-Briggs indicator and realized that arithmetic required me to use my inferior function—the one we never develop fully. My skills lay in the interpretive field, not the literal and measurable.

Recently I was delighted by an account of a classroom incident in Kathleen Norris' *The Cloister Walk*. She describes her reaction as a child to her teacher's statement that "two plus two is always four." Norris had spontaneously responded, "That can't be," and the class had laughed. She discovered years later that in different forms of higher math her insight was valid. A. E. Houseman expresses the plight of the imaginative view:

> To think that two and two are four
> And neither five nor three,
> The heart of man has long been sore
> And long 'tis like to be.

Being unaware of other dimensions of math that might supply me with some consolation, I worked out my frustration that summer by once more playing with words:

> He who hath the new math
> Will never answer wrong in clath
> For he shall know by intuition
> What others learn with imprecision.

Although I had completed a music major and was supposed to have taught the violin at a high school part time during my first year of teaching grammar school, it didn't happen. During my second year of teaching the fourth grade, I gave violin lessons to one little girl after school once a week. It seemed a shame that the Catholic grammar schools didn't have instrumental music programs like the one I had experienced in my own grammar school days. The choral music taught was mainly for use at liturgical functions. Later, as I taught up through the different grades and into high school, it became evident that science and math were considered the important subjects, the arts and humanities taking the back seat. I questioned the value of this emphasis, since I had found a truly spiritual dimension in the arts—particularly music and literature. It was strange that schools founded especially for religious formation should neglect the arts. But it was a direction that followed that of our Western technological world. Monsignor O'Reilly, a deeply spiritual man and an outstanding physicist who taught at our college, once remarked that the church seemed to join the world at the very moment that "the world was going down the tubes." His insights were usually valid.

The next summer it was time for me to make final vows. Before profession day on August 15, the feast of the Assumption of Mary, it was customary to make a lengthy retreat with the others of our "reception," the group that we had entered with. That year a book entitled *The Sins of the Just* had been published. The author suggested that those who considered themselves to be just or righteous should take a second look at themselves to see if a pharisaical slip might be showing. A number of my group had read or were reading the book. The superior in charge of the group felt that some of us were being negatively influenced by the book, and were "thinking too much," like Cassius in *Julius Caesar*. The situation reminded me of a story by Chesterton about a ship whose captain always sailed in the opposite direction from his intended destination. When a newly acquired crew member pointed this out, the saying went about that "There's a Mind on board." The sisters directing the retreat must have felt the same way, only they evidently had the feeling that there was more than one mind aboard. Each day at our common conference, the director would suggest that we pray and reflect carefully before taking the step of making final vows. One of my group paraphrased her daily message as, "If you don't like it—get out." Was someone in charge hoping to discover the minds on board before the ship sailed? A few of us took advantage of the swimming pool at the retreat site, daily swimming to the middle of the pool to discuss these conjectures in private. But we all ended up making final vows, so the alleged "minds" must have slipped in after all.

After the long retreat, we had a shorter retreat at the novitiate house. Since it was the last week of July, the new assignments had been published. We were called in one by one and told what our personal mission was for the fall. However, because we were on retreat, we weren't told about anyone else's—the people in our present house, our friends, etc. Before I entered, my mother had said, "Remember, you're going to be living with a bunch of women." Whether this was a last ditch argument of indirect dissuasion, or a valuable insight to take with me hadn't been clear at the time. Now I think it was both. Experience taught me that living with "a bunch of women" was not for sissies, but also that it made a big difference who the women in a particular house were. We often quoted to each other the familiar phrase, "It's not the cage, it's the birds in it that make the difference." It was upsetting not to know who we would be living with and where our friends might be. In a burst of bravery and sisterly sympathy, I approached the sister in charge of our retreat to lay our plight before her. She just said, "Well, my superior hasn't said anything about it—she probably didn't want to disturb your recollection." It seemed to me that not knowing was the disturbance. The implications of her remark reminded me of the time I had revealed to one of the novitiate superiors that I was interested in getting to know a certain sister in our group better, thinking we might be friends. She told me to forget about such feelings; she herself hadn't had contact with any of her own group for years—not since they left the novitiate.

I had a feeling that the sister in charge of the retreat would probably have the same view or non-view, of the situation. Providentially, I had a cleaning task during the retreat, which culminated in dumping a wastebasket in the provincial common room. Just above the wastebasket the entire mission list had been posted, showing everyone's assignments. From that day until the end of the retreat I offered "take out orders" to individual members of my group. They gave me names of individual sisters or convents, and I would then empty the wastebasket slowly enough to memorize the locations of the names on the list. It was a little like

"Mission Impossible," but fortunately the list didn't self-destruct, so I returned each day for another look.

As for my personal assignment, the retreat directress told me that I was being missioned to San Francisco. As she spoke, I envisioned myself being catapulted over the Golden Gate Bridge into what my family in Fresno called "The City." It had always been a magical place to me, a cosmopolitan city where people always dressed up as though every day were a formal, special occasion. The hills, the many storied buildings, the trolley cars, Fisherman's Wharf, the Cliff House—all were exciting features not found in the towns of the broad flatland of the inland San Joaquin Valley. My grandmother had lived in the Bay Area most of her life and told us stories that I mostly dismissed as being "old"—regrettably. I had been there a number of times, but rarely to stay overnight, and never for such a prolonged period as a school year,

At the end of the summer I wasn't catapulted north, but arrived by plane. A practical sister picked me up, as one of her tasks that morning. On the way to the convent she stopped at Sears to pick up some nuts, bolts, and nails for something she was repairing. The stop was quite a contrast to my romantic ideas of the place. We arrived at the convent in time for lunch. I picked up a sandwich in the kitchen and joined the others at the table. An older sister who had grown up in San Francisco and was well known there was holding forth. She spoke with the rather Bostonian pronunciation characteristic of some San Franciscans. When she came to a brief pause, I ventured a meek remark. She turned toward me as if examining a foreign object and said dismissively, "I don't know you." It felt that she was welcome to inquire about me, but evidently decided that it wasn't worth bothering about, and resumed her story. Had I wandered into Wonderland and met the Red Queen? As I finished my lunch I felt as Alice must have when she downed the draft that made her shrink. Years later that same sister was quite friendly to me, having learned who I was, but God had definitely gifted her with a formidable personality.

Star of the Sea (one of the titles of the Virgin Mary) was the name of
the school where I was to teach the seventh grade. Neither the school
nor the convent lived up to the beauty of the name. The convent was a
box-like structure of three stories situated on a busy corner. However, it
had a roof with a view of the whole city and beyond. This became my
favorite place. Once I made an uneducated attempt to create a kite out
of newspaper to fly from the roof, but I could never get it off the
ground, except by picking it up. The roof provided a view of the Golden
Gate Bridge, the tops of the trees of Golden Gate Park, "Lone
Mountain"—a Catholic college for women—and St. Ignatius Church,
next to the University of San Francisco. These were the only places in
the vast landscape of city hills that I could identify. Since the kite didn't
fly, I tried a poem:

> Bee hive, city of hills
> You dare much by your braceleted buildings
> Wound around each mound or mountain.
> Multidimensional, you pose as Picasso's own
> But marked more as Mary's
> With promontories of promise,
> Citadels of Christendom:
> A lone mountain, a soldier's fort
> Guard the Great Gates.

The principal of the grammar school had grown up in San Francisco,
as had Red Queen, and she pronounced "trash cans" in a most fascinating way when she gave the children directions about keeping the yard
clean. She gave the "a" such a broad sound that it came off as "tray-aysh
cans." I didn't follow all of the other details of her talk too carefully,
hoping to hear the phrase again—indeed, she repeated it quite often.
Although I supported her trash can policy, I did not live up to her
expectations in some other matters, such as writing my lesson plans in

minute detail. I found some of her practices slavish and inhibitive for me personally. One day she confronted me in the convent. I listened to her as well as I could, but whether I was suffering from a lack of excitement or just good sense that day, I told her truthfully that if I went along with her suggestions, I might end up being just like her, and that I didn't feel that would be the right thing for me. The right thing for me at that moment probably would have been to say "Thank you" and keep quiet, but my statement had an unexpected effect on her. She didn't seem to know what to say next, so our conversation ended for the day.

In those days we were supposed to be generally friendly, but not to have what were called "particular friendships"—which in effect meant no significant friendships at all. The idea seemed to be that taking a vow of celibacy meant that one was to be detached from people and relationships. Although detachment is a Christian virtue with a specific definition, indifference is quite another thing and quite compatible with superficial friendliness. Somewhere down the line the two ideas must have been confused.

However, two elderly sisters who lived there appeared to be exempt from the prohibition. Because one was tall and the other short, they were nicknamed "Mutt and Jeff" and were seen regularly doing things together. I wondered if it was because of their age or because of their virtue that their friendship was generally accepted—maybe both? The tall one was said to have bathed in her underwear, so as to avoid looking at anything indecent. The short one had allegedly let a stranger into the parlor and left him alone in order to go to her room to get him a holy card. A few valuable items disappeared with him. Perhaps these activities were considered to be virtues—examples of modesty and piety. On the other hand, maybe the two friends were considered to be harmless enough to warrant special privileges. Or perhaps a bit of eccentricity exempted one from the usual pattern? I wasn't sure. Little did I know as I wondered about their friendship, that I was to meet a sister that year who would turn out to be a life-long friend.

The convent housed at least twenty-five sisters, most of them older and more experienced than I. At dinner the younger sisters had tasks at which we took turns—dishing up the food, serving it, washing dishes, cleaning the dining room, etc. Unless it was a special occasion, we all kept silence at dinner while one of us read from a spiritual book. The dining room, like the chapel, was designated a place of silence ordinarily, even when we cleaned it. Once when I was feeling particularly cheerful, I hummed a piece of music softly as I wiped off the table. An older sister heard me as she passed the door, stepped in, sidled up to me and said, "Hum in your heart, dear."

When I took my turn at dishing up the food in the kitchen, my future friend was there to carry the dishes to the table. I was quite nervous, hoping I could dish up correctly and quickly enough. She, on the other hand, stood there calmly as if it didn't make the least bit of difference how long it took or if any of the older sisters would be either pleased or annoyed. Years later, it was no surprise to find out that she was a strong "P" on the Myers-Briggs test, whereas I have always been an anticipatory, anxious "J." At the time, I found her equanimity magical.

We began to spend time together on walks and in talks on the roof. One day I received an invitation to attend the first vow ceremony of a friend of mine who had entered the Dominican Sisters in San Rafael. Any activity out of the ordinary required permission from the superior. The day happened to coincide with a community outing. Many times the youngest sisters were assigned to an "inning" to answer the phone, etc. on outing days. So my request was denied; I was put on phone and door duty. My friend opted out of the group activity, so we both stayed home. I told her about my plight. She offered solid support by suggesting that we avenge my disappointment by searching the house for caches of candy. (On special occasions, boxes of candy appeared in the superior's hands, only to disappear at the end of the hour of recreation we were allowed). The candy must have been in the locked cupboards. Our only prize was an empty Milk of Magnesia bottle. In a seizure of creative spontaneity, we dashed up to the roof and I reduced the bottle to tiny pieces of blue glass by hitting it against a low wall. We then mixed the glass in with the gravel evenly to give it a blue-gray effect. Ten years later I returned to that roof and could still see tiny bits of blue, visible reminders of the fruitless candy search that day.

Being neither elderly nor highly virtuous in the eyes of the superior, I must have been suspected of being in danger of forming a "particular friendship," because I was moved at the end of that year. I didn't know, of course, when I packed my trunk, left it in San Francisco and traveled to Los Angeles for summer school, that I wouldn't return. My friend and I traveled south on the same train—a fine experience of viewing many miles of California.

That summer I attended classes and lived at the Doheny Campus of the college in downtown Los Angeles, and my friend stayed on the hill at the original campus above Brentwood. We got together when we could, but on the missioning day at the end of the summer I learned that I was changed from San Francisco to teach at a grammar school in Los Angeles. The price was high for friendship. It would be another year before my friend and I would meet again. That fall at my new mission I wrote another poem:

October: Intimations of Mortality
I bit into an apple yesterday;
The firm fresh fruit
Turned my eyes toward autumn trees
Aflame with amber light
Found only in the fall.

I felt time touch me with
A far-off hand.
Yet having found a fullness in the summer sun,
I longed to look upon its light a moment more,

But the redness of the apple
Drove my glance hard home
Toward the harvest.

At the parish grammar school in Los Angeles, I taught the seventh grade again. We went across the street to the church for the six o'clock morning Mass during the week. The priest was invariably late, so we usually waited outside in the cold for about fifteen or twenty minutes. Why the Mass time wasn't changed to fit his rising habits, or why we didn't start across the street a bit later was a mystery to me. On Sundays we were expected to attend more than one of the morning Masses so that people could see us as a presence in the parish. Actually, they couldn't see very much of us since we sat in the front pew and were wearing full habits. It occurred to me that we could have just propped up some stuffed habits for at least one of the liturgies, but had the good sense not to mention it.

A priest came to our convent chapel once a week to hear our confessions. It wasn't always the same priest, and, of course, he didn't know who the person was that confessed to him. I had always felt that the impersonal aspect threatened to reduce the sacrament to becoming just a perfunctory routine. I wondered what kind of experience it must be to listen to a series of perhaps innocuous confessions of nameless nuns. My imagination got the better of me, and I wondered if it might pep up the priest's day if I claimed to have done in my grandmother or carried out some other outrageous act, but then realized I was thinking sacrilegiously and wondered—should I confess the thought? On at least one occasion, I had mentioned something to a priest in confession that seemed to have shocked him. One had to be honest, but careful.

To my chagrin, my wayward tendencies inherited through original sin had not abated after all this time. When the superior assigned me the task of teaching choir in a darkened church with no keyboard instrument nor pitch pipe available, I had the effrontery to tell her that

I had majored in music and knew that one needed these things to perform correctly. She had no musical training, but told me that the sister who led the choir before me had taught the children by rote. Teaching music by rote without a musical instrument was not something I had had any experience with. Another area in which I fell short was the proper cleaning of the convent dining room, which was my assigned charge. The music encounter and the dust under the large china closet in the dining room seemed to have affected the superior strongly. I went up to my second floor room after school one Friday as usual, and a sister came by my room to say, "Sister is cleaning your charge." I said a grateful prayer and pretended I hadn't heard the news. As was my custom, I placed my personal copy of the diocesan paper on the bed, put my feet up on it and continued reading a book that I had started that was well written. (Happily, the diocesan paper was later upgraded and is now timely, well written, and worth reading.)

During that year I began to realize that the superiors had a great deal of power, controlling not only the purse strings, but the phone lines, and the car keys. Reflecting upon the contrast between this unholy thought and the ideals of religious life, I missed the last stair step one day and dislocated a bone in my foot. My sister Donna lived in the area at that time and drove me to the doctor, bringing my young niece Francesca and nephew Christopher with her. Upon hearing that I was suffering pain from a bone in my foot, my nephew asked, "But how did that bone get into Aunt Mona's foot?"

Again my stay at a mission was short, lasting only one year. Perhaps I was moved because another superior suspected I was secretly "against the government," but in those days one never knew. Although the superior and I didn't see eye to eye on some things, I was surprised one day to see her walking directly toward me, as if she might not stop, in the sacristy of the chapel where I was putting away vestments. For a split second I thought a major confrontation was at hand, but then I realized it was myself I saw, reflected in the long mirror the priest uses for vesting. She and I were about the same height, eye to eye in one sense, and of course we wore the same habit. The mirror image effect might have provided some material for reflection on the shadow aspects of myself, but I was not to become familiar with that Jungian concept until years later.

The following summer I met my friend from San Francisco again at the college where she worked in the library. We enjoyed some time together between my classes and her duties. When I was studying in the library one morning she invited me to a coffee break, whispering biblically, "My beeves and fatlings are killed." (They turned out to be doughnuts and coffee cake.) At the end of the summer, we traveled in different directions again—she back to San Francisco and I to my new assignment in San Diego.

The convent in San Diego was an old Victorian house that had been added on to. It contained mysterious dark corners and closets and unusual rooms for baths. There were skylights that opened to the air above each of the tubs, into which visiting voyeur sea gulls and other birds occasionally peeked during one's bath. My room was on the second floor and gave a view of the freeway. The desk in my room was in front of the window and I usually spent some time after school hours looking out, sometimes attempting a poem:

> ### View
> I have become accustomed to this scene,
> A few palm trees and unpruned bushes,
> Beyond that, the freeway,
> Then the dark and distant park.
>
> Reflected in my desk top,
> Seagulls circle,
> Spiral to deep dimensions
> In glass and sky.

That year I again taught seventh grade. We had a Christmas program at which each class performed. I decided on a choral speech rendition of "King John's Christmas," a narrative poem by A. A. Milne that begins:

King John was not a good man;
He had his little ways
And sometimes no one spoke to him
For days and days and days.

The poem goes on to relate that the only Christmas cards King John received were those he sent to himself. He kept hoping for a present, in particular his favorite toy, "An India rubber ball." The high point of the tale is a complete surprise that changes his Scrooge-like attitude. By accident, a child in the street bounces a ball too high and it sails into his room through his window to delight him. Each seventh grader had a part in the production. I had assigned the task of carrying the rubber ball to a boy who didn't seem capable of contributing much else. Unfortunately, I overestimated his abilities. As the climax of the play approached, the chorus of voices rose in excitement:

And through the window,
Round and red,
There hurtled by his royal head
And bounced upon the royal bed
An India rubber ball!

An ominous silence followed. Then somebody backstage half-heartedly threw a sock of Christmas candy onto the stage, which landed with a dull "plop," instead of the bouncing sound and dramatic sight of the intended red ball. Fortunately for the boy that was responsible, I couldn't find him back stage afterward. When we all walked out of the hall into the cold December night, I found myself near a group of priests who were having a good laugh about the sock. The boy who had "socked it to us" had disappeared in the dark and then was absent from class the next day. Perhaps his perceptions had been sharpened by the experience. Education takes many forms.

The next summer I took a class in linguistics and made contact with a book company that offered fifty percent off on its new grammar books to any school that implemented the new program. The official name of this approach was "transformational grammar." It reminded me of the new math in that all the intricacies of the process were revealed to the student. Somehow both methods resembled a parent's attempt to make a small child understand all the moral and psychological angles behind the requirements of good behavior, as opposed to just saying, "Do it because I said so."

In my experience, the rules of language really didn't make any logical sense; somewhere along the line people had just arbitrarily decided that certain sounds uttered in certain ways communicated certain meanings. Furthermore, English has borrowed extensively from other tongues. To invite children to know and appreciate all the underpinnings of English didn't seem as important as just teaching them what had been determined to be correct by people who had been born before they were. In any case, our school took up the book offer. Since I was the only one educated in the new approach, I taught English to five different grades the next year—third through eighth. The books had beautiful pictures and good poetry, which I thought outweighed the abstract transformational theories.

That year a number of religious communities decided to begin programs directed toward modifying the religious habit. Various experimental habits started to appear. An adventuresome sister in our house volunteered to wear one. I remember her standing on a low table in the parlor while someone pinned the hem of her skirt high enough to look modern, but low enough to hide her knees appropriately. The concern for propriety recalled a scene some years before when I attended a gathering of sisters at which one of the vital questions under discussion was whether or not we should chew gum in public. Was gum chewing inappropriate for a person wearing a religious habit? Now that the religious habit was being modernized, I wondered whether the change would also lead to a rash of publicly gum-chewing nuns.

By the middle of the school year I decided that it was time for me to choose a modified habit—a short veil, and short skirt, primarily. When I attended the NCEA in San Francisco, my sister Donna happened to be living there, having moved north from the Los Angeles area. She is an artist and had been involved in costume design in college. Her opinion was that our congregation's traditional habit had beautiful lines. The only artistic choice was to either keep the full habit or change into modern clothes. The modified habit was merely a truncated version of an aesthetically pleasing design. However, in spite of her theory, she shopped with me for a blouse, skirt, etc.

Meanwhile, I continued to wear the full habit, having decided to change the day after school was out in June, so that my students and I wouldn't have to adjust to such a thing in midstream, especially since I met with five different classes. Maybe I was just being overly self-conscious like the sister in the joke who went swimming and was seen in her swim suit by a little boy in her class whose only comment was, "Sister! I've never seen you without your glasses!"

Besides the changes occurring in long-standing religious congregations, new groups of religious began forming. Some wore completely modern dress and engaged in new forms of ministry. One new community of sisters lived in our parish. Our sister in the experimental habit met them and after awhile, both she and I visited them regularly. They shared their stories with us and played popular songs on the phonograph like "The Girl from Ipanema."

In the spring the new community invited several of our houses to a potluck dinner. The meal included a number of dishes and beverages, including wine, which we ordinarily didn't serve in our communities.

Most people left about 10:30. A few of us stayed later and wandered into the backyard. There was a pack of cigarettes on the outside table. Did some of them smoke? Responding to a dare, we all tried one. I had smoked a little in college before entering, but not in public. When one of my college English teachers had required us to write a short story, I felt it was a burdensome, nearly impossible task. I dressed in black, closed my bedroom door, and smoked furiously to vent my frustration. It didn't help the story, which was a pitiful attempt at a plot involving roses that St. Therese dropped down from heaven to inspire the various characters to action. The idea came from a sentimental hymn to St. Therese, the namesake of our parish: "Drop down just one little rose— the rose we need today." I probably could have benefited from having one of those roses drop on me to inspire me to give up on the story and try something else.

Within the next few days after the potluck, our superior received a Los Angeles call from a sister in charge of schools, who said, "I hear there's trouble down there." The superior countered, "I wouldn't say that." Then she heard another voice, "I'm on the other line, Sister." It was the voice of the provincial superior who had been monitoring the call. The provincial said that she had been informed that three of us had been seen "drinking and smoking in front of the other communities." The three had been the sister in modified habit and I and another of our sisters who lived in a nearby convent.

On Palm Sunday the three of us were put on a plane for Los Angeles. Escorted to the provincialate, we were placed in separate rooms to be questioned by the provincial. While I was awaiting questioning, I considered making up a more colorful, exciting account, but just told the simple truth when the time came. A sister who had been in the novitiate with me saw me in the hall and said, "If they're questioning the three of you, we're all in trouble." I learned later that she smoked secretly. The next summer my room was above hers in the college residence building. A couple of cohorts must have joined her for a smoke. I heard voices and could smell smoke. I made a sign out of a large piece of cardboard and wrote, "NO SMOKING" in bold print, then lowered it from my window on a piece of string to a level where they could see it. The talking suddenly stopped, and at least one person choked a little.

The three of us survived the Palm Sunday questioning and returned to San Diego. Easter vacation came, then went too quickly. The time after Easter is usually busy. Both teachers and students begin to long for the end of the school year, which entails completing course material and preparing to leave the classrooms in order. The day after school ended was still my target date for changing to the short habit. I had by then worn the full habit for ten years, and had grown accustomed to it. The afternoon of the day before the change, I was so nervous that I almost ran a red light in downtown San Diego. It seemed an ironic contrast to my trembling candle of years ago. The third member of our interrogated trio changed the same day. Someone took a picture of the three of us. Looking back at the picture, I know my sister had been right about the lack of artistic options. We looked like refugees from another country. However, we didn't realize this and were spared the experience that a friend of mine had when she adopted a modified habit. One of her blood sisters, who had joined a different religious order and still wore the full habit, greeted her with, "You look just like a drowned rat!" upon seeing her in the modified garb.

More changes followed the choice of modern dress. The method of assigning new missions for the next year took a different form. Instead of being read out loud at the end of the summer, all new assignments were listed and mailed to the local superior, who informed the sisters in her house before the end of the school year. Whether because of my nefarious activities or because I had expressed an interest in teaching high school, I was sent the next year to a girls' high school in Los Angeles. By the end of that summer I had acquired a second major in English; the number of classes I had voluntarily taken had accumulated.

Shortly before I began teaching in the high school, my new principal called me to say that she had three problem classes to distribute and asked me to choose one of them. The classes were drama, yearbook, and something called Metromedia. Still suffering from the memories of the sock flop, and mystified by the term "Metromedia," I chose the yearbook reluctantly. It seemed enough of a challenge to teach high school English for the first time without attempting to do the yearbook, but it was a scheduled class instead of an after school activity, so it wasn't an additional assignment after a full day. Since I had been on the yearbook staff in my own high school, it was not entirely unfamiliar to me.

Soon after that, I called the school and asked the principal if I might pick up the textbooks I would be using. She asked me to stop by her office when I came by because she wanted to see my face when she told me something. I presented my face when I arrived. She said they really had no one else to teach the drama class, so that class would be mine also. In those days the idea of saying "No, thank you" wasn't encouraged. I consoled myself with the thought that I had directed a second classroom play in San Diego based on *Alice in Wonderland*. It had gone rather well and the seventh graders had enjoyed the silly lines, for example, "Give me a ham sandwich—I'm feeling faint."

Shortly before the first day of school the principal phoned again. This time she evidently didn't want to see my face. She informed me that the sister scheduled to teach the Metromedia class felt that the class was too much of a burden for her in addition to her other tasks. At that point I could second her feeling, but she outranked me. The words of my German novice mistress applied to a sister of my age and experience level: "Remember—feelings don't count."

The Metromedia class consisted of seventy-five juniors and seniors who met in an extra large classroom. The sister who had planned the class was no longer at the school, and in those days we had no official syllabus for any class. I realized that media included films, so I concentrated on that angle. Following the dictum that we inexperienced teachers thought up at my first assignment, "Learn while you teach," I concocted a self-study film course and shared what I learned with the class. The trick was to always have a film handy. I explored the AV sections of the local libraries and sent for whatever films were available at the diocesan office. Much of the preparation for the class consisted in hauling movies back and forth. In those days we used projectors and 16 millimeter film. I learned how to splice, coax, and pray over uncooperative film loops.

The drama class was composed of freshmen through seniors. What to do with such disparate groups? I broke them into appropriate levels and had them do group work on different short plays. The groups took turns reading and performing parts of plays while I tried not to laugh or cry at the wrong times. Since this motley group could not possibly put on a play for the school, I held open tryouts for a female version of "Twelve Angry Men." The twelve girls playing the parts of angry women sometimes did the play one better by bursts of anger at things the playwright hadn't intended. Although they were mostly seniors and therefore supposedly the more mature in the school, I had to deal with weeping young women and ruffled feathers more often than I cared to. One of the performances was on a school night, so I worked up courage enough to ask the principal if the cast might be allowed to come to school a bit later the next day. The principal said definitely not, and seemed to think it inappropriate of me to ask. Surprisingly, the play came off rather well, but the players might have been mentally absent for part of the next day. (At least one teacher wasn't quite there.)

In the second semester the English Department decided to try an experimental approach involving a "modular" scheduling of a top group of sophomores. Why I was chosen as their teacher was a mystery to me. Maybe it was because I was seen as a likely target for almost anything by this time. Having had not much background in many of the things I was teaching—except English classes—what was one more? To vary the special program I instituted a Mickey Mouse Day once a month. The class brought Mickey Mouse hats, we sang the traditional

"M-I-C-K-E-Y M-O-U-S-E" club song and then watched and discussed some of the short animated films I had discovered in my private film study. One was a little gem called "Why Man Creates." In one part an Arab shouts, "Allah be praised! I've invented the zero!" Another says, "What?" The first answers, "Nothing, nothing." Another film shows the Los Angeles of the future as a large parking lot. There are so many cars that no roads are left. People live in cars, stacked one upon the other. The wealthy live on the top layer, and the poorest on ground level. Helicopters fly constantly above, taking orders for food and other necessities. The orders are written on flags sent up on pulleys by people on various car levels.

Having complained about the principal at the end of that year, I was then missioned to a coeducational high school north of Los Angeles. I found the area distinctly provincial compared to Los Angeles itself, which, although smoggy and sprawling, did have many available cultural opportunities. But there was one distinct advantage—my friend from San Francisco had been sent to the same school the previous year and was still there. We were both wearing the modified habit by that time and enjoyed saying things like, "It's nice to be seeing so much more of you lately."

By the early 1970s, the Mass and all hymns were in English. I missed the symbolic universality and mystique of the Latin. Knowing that Masses all over the world were being said in the same language held a numinosity for me. The fact that it was a "dead language," no longer utilitarian, gave it the aura of a sacred language. Because the beautiful Gregorian chant and traditional hymns in Latin had been replaced for the most part, by sentimental music and insipid texts, I tried to practice detachment. The Mass wasn't just an aesthetic experience; after all, we were celebrating the sacrificial death of Jesus for the salvation of all. Perhaps the distress allowed me to "fill up the sufferings of Christ" in some small way—or was I rationalizing, in the manner of one coping with an undesirable situation?

The concept of having "group government" instead of a local superior was becoming a reality in a number of houses. I thought it a good idea to make decisions together, although in some experimental meetings I had observed that coming to consensus wasn't easy. When we first started discussing matters in order to come to a common decision, we found discussion most difficult—we didn't know how to talk to each other openly and honestly with ease after so many years of unquestioning silent obedience. Many of us felt that we had to come to such a meeting fully armed, ready to be either confronted or overlooked. The extraverts did most of the talking. Some of us came with prepared texts, as if giving a speech, and some seemed to have resolved to say nothing unless forced into it. Expressions of strong feelings were frowned upon, so many times we spoke to each other with what today has been called "dysfunctional civility," not really revealing our most important concerns.

In the high school convent where I was living, we had a choice between having group government or a local superior. One of our number felt that others of us needed a superior, and she was glad to volunteer. There was an old saying that anyone who really wanted to be a superior shouldn't be chosen to hold that office. I'm not sure how often that sage advice was followed. Some years before I entered the community, the superiors held the title of "Mother" and many of them took it seriously, treating the others like children. Frequently they bought little trinkets, usually religious ones, for the sisters. I stored up a number of these unwanted items and later gave them away to other people who probably didn't want them either. With these considerations in mind, we out-voted the would-be superior and put ourselves at the mercy of group government for better or worse.

That being my first teaching experience in a coeducational high school, I began to notice the great importance attached to the sports program, particularly football. When I attended high school myself, I saw the football games as central to the spirit of the school, and to the fall social life of the students. From the perspective of a teacher, however, the emphasis on winning, and the time athletes spent outside the classroom seemed disproportionate in the light of religious and academic values. Sometimes boundaries became blurred, as evidenced by the fact that the current coach attempted to integrate prayer and football practice by having the team lie on the gym floor shouting out the rosary to improve breath control.

In my second year at the school, I was asked to moderate the school newspaper. That year I taught senior English and we read Orwell's *Animal Farm* as one of the novels. The seniors who were the top staff members on the newspaper were creative and talented, sometimes a dangerous combination for high school journalism. Some of them wrote a parody of the *Animal Farm* plot, satirizing the school administration—no real names used of course. It was well done, and I let them use it, mistakenly thinking that a school newspaper was an organ for student expression, not to be taken too seriously by adults.

The day that the edition was to be distributed, an emergency faculty meeting was called. The papers had been confiscated, with the exception of enough for the faculty, who were seated around the library in a circle. The principal passed one paper to each teacher; he then directed everyone to read silently through the article. I was seated across the circle from the principal. After the reading, he asked the faculty for comments, and a low-grade Joan of Arc scene took place, fortunately without the actual fire. The fact that the characters in the piece were so easily identifiable indicated that perhaps the students were on to something, and had even communicated their thoughts and feelings to some extent, in spite of the dire consequences for the edition and the inexperienced moderator. The principal contacted my religious superiors and evidently they all agreed that I was needed in a high school in Los Angeles the following year. So both the senior perpetrators and I left the school after their graduation.

By that time, a few musicians had begun to turn out new liturgical music, and had come up with hymns that were well worded and singable. One of them began "Yahweh is the God of my Salvation." The next lines were "I trust in Him and have no fear." Unfortunately, attempts to express modern trends in theology took a less creative turn. Some theological expressions began to sound like algebraic equations or complicated chemistry formulas. I imagined putting one of the worst to the music of the "Yahweh" song. The result: "Jesus is the summation of the concrete criteria by which we discern spirits—I trust in Him and have no fear, etc."

The next fall at the coed high school in Los Angeles I again taught English, including some specialty classes such as Fantasy in Literature and Science Fiction. In the fantasy class I gave a few assignments that took the students outside the classroom. One of these was to follow directions for a quest. I made up the first one, directing the questers to pass a number of wooden giants (telephone poles), turn right at the place of Magic Wands (transformers) and find the secret message Superman left under the letter "Q" (a message in a phone booth telephone book). Then the students took turns developing quests by challenging each other with clues from some of the medieval lore we were reading. Unfortunately, the sight of students tracking imaginary creatures and treasures outside the classroom did not sit well with the administrators, so the project only lasted one semester. Singing songs to the Invisible Christmas Tree in a selected hallway seemed to fare better, but it was a project limited to a week or two before Christmas.

The next semester I was faced with the challenge of teaching a class made up almost entirely of sophomore boy athletes. The class met after lunch, when either the sugar levels had built up too much excitement, or the number of sandwiches for lunch had produced sluggish tendencies to nap. In an attempt to benefit from the boys' sports training, I lined them all up on bleachers near the football field and hurled quiz questions at them one by one, right down the line. This approach worked for a limited time.

One day when I arrived to open the door for class, I found a number of boys grouped around one of their classmates who lay on his back on the floor of the corridor. His eyes were closed; his T-shirt was pulled up to reveal a red mark on his torso. His concerned friends rushed toward me, telling me he had fallen from the second floor railing. All were eager to run for help. I advised them to drag what was left of him into the classroom. The desks were arranged in a semicircle to facilitate discussion, with an area of open space in the middle of the floor. I told them to place him there, so I could keep an eye on him. We started class, and after about five minutes, he opened his eyes and sheepishly crawled to his seat. I had almost decided to go along with them—the period after lunch was one of the worst times for teachers and students alike. But the red mark under his T-shirt looked suspiciously like a self-inflicted slap.

That year I had the opportunity of attending a weekend workshop on teaching resistant students. The presenter challenged some traditional ideas by suggesting that perhaps the students shouldn't be the only ones allowed to give trouble in the classroom. I followed up some of his suggestions the next time I gave a test to the after-lunch group. Usually I walked around the room during a test. This time I varied the procedure by stepping gently on the foot of one of the regular perpetrators. Then I sidled up to another who was carefully writing down an answer and jiggled his arm slightly—just enough for him to make a squiggly line off into the margin. The boys were dumbfounded. I never tried it again. I think I was in danger of unbalancing their inner sensitivities by such barbarism.

Four

Quandries and Questions

Meanwhile the changes in religious life continued. More houses were opting for group government. Without a local superior in the house, groups had to decide together on their daily schedules of prayer, meal times, etc. For many years there had been a rule of silence in convents except on special occasions. The increasing freedom to go out without sister companions and to stay overnight in other convents seemed to foster more conversation, as did the time spent talking over group decisions. The rule of silence had encouraged many of us to go deeper into our own prayer, reflection, reading, and introspection in general. When silence times became less defined, we began to discover that we were not all in agreement about everything. The world as I saw it from my own room, in my own mind, might differ greatly from that of the sister living right next door to me.

Although the more silent, introspective time had called many of us to interior depth, much of our interpersonal development had remained on a parent to child level, the superiors giving parental directives and we obeying them. In a way it had been easier to have a superior running things. Freed from unpleasant decisions, we could either blame unfortunate consequences on her or develop coping mechanisms for survival. Some people became highly skilled at pleasing and/or manipulating superiors, much like women who faced similar situations in patriarchal marriages.

Underdeveloped psychological states surfaced in everyday life, as well as in group discussions. In houses where there was no official superior, certain sisters seemed to have a need to play mother. Frequently, the mothering took the form of attempts to return to tradition. Earlier on, it had been a custom on Saturday for each of us to clean her charge, the area in the house for which she was responsible. Even if we had Saturday college classes or other personal assignments, we had been expected to get up early or stay up late to fulfill that obligation. As schedules became more diversified, people chose their own times for chores. The would-be superiors, however, became very busy on Saturdays, making enough bustle and noise to induce sufficient guilt levels in others to abandon different pursuits in favor of cleaning. They expressed their wishes indirectly, but their underlying intent seemed to match C. S. Lewis's description of a newly married couple. One turns to the other and says, "Now here is my plan for you...."

In contrast to the would-be mothers, some sisters wanted to be mothered. In addition to playing into the hands of the "mothers," these people felt the need of great emotional outpouring and personal revelations at our meetings. After sharing traumatic moments of their lives, they would say, "I just feel that nobody understands me—that you don't really accept me. There's just something missing." I had felt that way myself on a number of occasions, but hated to think what might have happened, had I blurted those feeling out. Strangely enough, the more a person begs for attention, the less others are drawn to cooperate. In any case, such expectations were so idealistic that those who tried to respond found their best efforts could never satisfy the unmet needs.

An opposite reaction to the changes was a tendency to resist any authority. Sisters who took up this position became strongly independent individuals. At an earlier period, we had been encouraged to call everything "ours" instead of "mine," the choice of words reflecting the fact that we didn't own anything personally since all material goods were held in common. I didn't experience this vocabulary really catching on—"our desk," "our book," etc. I had wondered what the communal effect of saying, "our toothbrush" would have been. In any case, the rebels did daring things like appearing without the short veil, wearing bright colored clothing to large meetings, and making unexpected declarations at house meetings. An example that comes to mind: "I just want you all to know that I won't be joining you for common prayer. I'll be in my room at those times, following the gospel directives more closely—'When you pray, go to your room and close the door' etc." (I actually thought her statement a pretty good alternative, but was lacking overt rebel nerve.)

At that time the church generally became more conscious of the need to promote social justice by engaging in new forms of ministry directed at helping the marginal, the poor and the oppressed. A number of sisters who engaged in these good works became overzealous, expecting that everyone else in their house should be equally involved, despite the fact that others were still engaged in full-time teaching or nursing jobs. Van Kaam put it well:

> Perhaps one of the greatest temptations to misinterpret the voice of the Spirit in the religious community is the tendency of idealists to overwhelm others with their own excitement. I may silence the unique voices of the Spirit in others when I try to imbue them with my special social concern. I should guard against [disdaining] those...called to serve the Holy...as...scholars, artists, musicians or writers.

Although my father was on the editorial staff of a newspaper, I have never spent much time reading newspapers or news magazines. C. S. Lewis remarked that if anything really important happened, he would hear about it in the common room. There seemed to me to be more verbiage than news or serious thought in most news periodicals. A sister I lived with was deeply involved in the thrust toward social justice, and seeing me sitting on top of a newspaper that had been placed on a stool in the kitchen said, "I guess that's the only way you'll get the news—by osmosis."

As traditional structures in general were abandoned, experimental methods of prayer and liturgies developed. Instead of either a common meditation period or common prayer based on the hours of the Divine Office (selected psalms and responses), "shared prayer" emerged. Usually the structure was up to the person leading the prayers. Personal reflections, thoughts, and petitions were a major part of the ritual. People started passing around sea shells and flowers, often playing individually chosen musical selections in the background. A priest I had for class one summer said that he thought prayer was an expression of love. The "shared prayer" he had experienced seemed to be as inappropriate as making love in public. He compared formal liturgy and the divine office to ballroom dancing, an appropriate and elegant expression of a love relationship in public. He was of the opinion that people needed to spend a good deal of time in private individual prayer before participating in shared prayer in order that the communal forms being developed might preserve the depth and reverence characteristic of traditional liturgies.

Changing the liturgy into vernacular languages necessarily affected the universal symbolism afforded by the Latin Mass. Masses for specific groups began at this time. There were Masses for teenagers, for grammar school children, and even pumpkin Masses for first graders in order to capture their Halloween interest. It seemed that one Mass intended for all age groups in a parish would necessarily both please and displease the various age groups. Each would have to adapt in some way to the experience of the whole parish, but wasn't the give and take of that situation more realistic? I wondered how far this trend would go? Would there be Masses for tall and short, bald and beautiful? Perhaps the parish could be divided up ethnically. Would that help or hinder prejudicial tendencies? The new possibilities brought with them the problems of making responsible and appropriate choices in liturgy planning.

Long before the changes encouraged by the Second Vatican Council began, the ideals of religious life appeared to have fallen into a confusion between propriety and morality. Perhaps it was the result of modes of behavior inherited from the Victorian period or the influence of the many Irish priests and religious who came to this country, bringing with them a somewhat staid propriety that contrasted with the more informal behavior of Americans. Before entering the convent, I remember having visited the provincial of the order and having been given what was called "high tea"—something I had never experienced at home. In the novitiate we attended a class in table etiquette, including manners and the proper preparation of a formal meal. The group of three or four chosen to demonstrate for us on a little stage wore the habit perfectly and moved gracefully. In those days, silence at meals naturally promoted good manners. We had to give full attention to both passing the serving dishes and listening to the reading. One sister who sat next to me misjudged her strength in cutting a piece of meat. Part of it shot onto my plate. We continued as if it hadn't happened, but she quotes me as having whispered, "The next time you'd like to share something, I'd appreciate being asked first." Evidently no one else had noticed the impropriety at the table.

There was also a tendency to confuse perfectionism with holiness. I remember a sister whose charge was to set the table for the highest ranking superiors in the dining room of the novitiate house. She used a surveyor's precision in lining up the individual salt and pepper shakers. I wandered in when she was double checking them. She had crouched down so that her eyes were level with the table. At first I thought she was hiding from someone. Then I saw that she had closed one eye and was scrutinizing the shakers to be sure that not one would be a millimeter out of line. Whereas some people seemed challenged by that sort of thing, others became quite frustrated. One morning I was cleaning the dining room floor together with a broadly educated, experienced sister, who had entered after having attended a prestigious college where she graduated with significant honors. She winked at me and said, "Let's wax and polish this floor so it will dazzle them. Maybe a few will slip on the way in?" I took it as a delightful, minor verbal rebellion.

As the number of changes in religious life increased, the numbers entering decreased. Rather than reflecting on our own lived experience and pursuing a much needed reevaluation of religious life and the direction it was taking in our times, many congregations simply tried to put more effort into reviving methods that had worked well in the past, ignoring the many changes in the world. Ministries that we had begun, such as schools, hospitals and catechetical work, were eventually staffed mainly by lay people. The church had begun to confront the dualism and Jansenistic modes of thought that had given religious life a more exalted place than that of sacramental marriage or the call to a single Christian life. Christian ministry was now seen as being a task and privilege of all believers, not as the exclusive domain of clergy and religious.

Many saw the diminishing number of girls entering the convent as a vocation crisis that we had to do something about. Meetings were called to discuss the problem. In the mid-1980s I attended a regional meeting at which part of the agenda was a discussion of the dearth of vocations. The concerns shared reflected the facts that we were aging as a community, we weren't attracting young girls, and many of our numbers had left religious life. It seemed that we needed to make plans to ensure our continuance as a congregation. We came to no conclusions, but circled a number of times around the proverbial bush. Looking back, I had the feeling that we should have been taking a good look at the bush itself, perhaps as a symbol of our present reality.

The meeting left me with an ambivalent feeling, perhaps some frustration, and a lack of clarity. I summarized the ideas expressed in an "alternative minutes" for myself:

1. We are still struggling, but this should be cleared up soon.
2. Try to look more attractive.
3. Stop getting older.
4. Force people who are thinking of leaving to stay.
5. Go out and persuade the ones who have left to return.
6. Move into the future—why hang around in the now?

Looking back at these "minutes," I see that statement number six contained a kernel of truth. A number of current writers, reflecting on religious life, have suggested that to "hang around in the now" is exactly what we should be doing. Our time is a transition period that requires contemplative listening, rather than grandiose plans of action. Joan Chittister states that "the purpose of religious life is not survival; it is prophecy...to bring to visibility what is Good News for our time now, not to preserve a past long gone and no longer germane to the challenge of new questions." Barbara Fiand describes the present as "a time for courageous waiting." She suggests that we need to spend time in reflection, allowing the Spirit to broaden our perspectives, following Einstein's dictum: "No problem can be solved from the same consciousness that created it."

Thirteen years later I attended a similar meeting in a different region. One of the main items on the agenda was again related to the scarcity of new members. Many of the same questions were asked and many of the same solutions were suggested. By that time more of us had retired from active ministry, so financial concerns had been added to the problem of having fewer young sisters to carry on. One of the first questions addressed to the group was "What are the qualities you would expect of a candidate for religious life?" The length of the list that ended up on the sheet of butcher paper in the front of the room was staggering. I remembered another meeting years before when the question "What is a Sister of St. Joseph?" was asked. We were in small discussion groups, and I suggested that the most you could say was that a person had to be officially a member of the congregation to be a Sister of St. Joseph. One member of the group was completely disgusted with me (maybe more were, but didn't speak up). She thought I should have rattled off a list of virtues of some sort. She left the congregation soon after that, leaving me still an official member and definitely without a long list.

During the meeting I stared at the list on the wall and wondered what would have happened if all of us had been tested for these admirable virtues and skills. Would we all be here? I had made a habit by now of creating alternative minutes for myself and wrote "next step—test every one in this room for these criteria to see if we all belong." Since we met late in October, the familiar phrase "We need new blood" sounded like a Halloween sentiment to me. We rehashed the number of retired members versus the number of new members, and in a macabre Halloween spirit I wrote, "Liquidate those who can't work in order to solve the financial problem." When it came to discussing publicity, making ourselves known through various programs, the internet, etc., the word "exposure" was used repeatedly. I began envisioning cabaret performances and other questionable forms of revelation. By that time the meeting was over and my imagination was exhausted for that day.

We seemed to have been spinning around the same bush that we circled over a decade ago. Fortunately, our province had launched a study focusing on the vows and the nature of religious life, to be discussed throughout the year. All of us were involved, each choosing a group that had decided to tackle the subject from a specific angle. We were availing ourselves of many current insightful works on the subject—Schneiders, Chittister, Fiand, O'Murchu, and others.

Some years ago, I had discovered Richard Rohr's work by listening to a tape entitled "Are We Sent or Are We Just Going?" His point was that the original Christian communities were made up of people drawn together and intimately sharing their lives and beliefs. It was their own faith and unity that impelled them to go out and share the Good News and minister to others. He suggested that we as a church, particularly the clergy and religious, were focusing so much on ministry, doing for others, that we no longer realized that the whole ministry project should be an outgrowth of a vibrant spirit of Christian love fueled by unity with one another, rather than a number of Lone Rangers or Rangerettes riding out from lives of isolated perfectionism. To be sent out by the Spirit to share what a vibrant community already shares was the original Christian model.

If it seemed important to reconnect ministry with Christian community, perhaps it was even more necessary to reflect on how people come to be members of a Christian community. In the church as a whole, this study of the history of evangelization resulted in the adult catechesis now formalized into the RCIA program. But what about those drawn to religious life? Is it appropriate to launch huge recruitment programs as if religious life were a form of the military?

In the 1950s, when there were many Catholic high schools for girls mainly staffed by sisters, individual congregations actively encouraged girls to enter. There was even rivalry between different groups of religious for candidates. I attended a co-instructional high school. The girls' side was run by sisters, the boys' by brothers. A different group of sisters staffed our parish school. I joined their sodality, a group dedicated to Mary, open to any teenage girl in the parish. In order to attend the reception and vow ceremony of the parish sisters' congregation, four of us had to skip school on Friday to travel to Los Angeles—a daring thing for me, since it was the first and only time I was illegally absent from high school. The sisters who taught us had the handicap of having a motherhouse in the East. They wouldn't count the trip to

Southern California as an excused absence, so we had to resort to a covert, underground plan. I felt as if I were sneaking off to cheer a rival school's volleyball team.

At the time I entered, large groups of girls from Catholic high schools entered together each year. There were sixty-eight in my original group on the first day. Whole volleyball teams entered from some girls' schools. Although we were encouraged not to speak of our personal families after entrance, in order to concentrate on our newly chosen life, girls from high schools conducted by the congregation tended to retain their identities as being from their former schools. There seemed to be almost a transference of the team spirit involved in playing sports to the "team" of religious life. When the post-conciliar changes in religious life began, some of the team mystique disappeared. A number of women who had initially experienced the presence and support of large groups left religious life during those years.

Congregational religious life does include a communal aspect, but a religious vocation is a truly personal call. Diarmuid O'Murchu writes, "The choice for celibacy…is not really a choice. It is the consequence of a call that is essentially mystical…. It only makes sense to those who can accept that a new reign of God operates in the world and lures people into options and lifestyles that leave them with no choice other than [to] respond affirmatively." Of the communal aspect he states, "A celibacy whose primary function is the enhancement of love and intimacy must be grounded in the lived experience of a community." All in all, it seemed that the idea of a vocation as a personal call from the Holy Spirit needed to be reconsidered in the midst of the anxiety caused by the diminishing numbers of religious vocations. O'Murchu suggests that a Christian community dimension is essential to religious life, but that the call itself is a personal invitation from the Holy Spirit, not subject to a broad recruitment program initiated by the members of religious congregations. As Joan Chittister wrote, "Religious life to be valid does not require a cast of thousands."

I spent the next fifteen years teaching English in several coeducational high schools in the Los Angeles Archdiocese. The students' reading levels had been dropping for a number of years. English departments attempted to address the problem by offering high interest, selective classes such as science fiction, fantasy, mythology, and existential writers, etc. Courses with titles such as "Power Reading" were introduced. As time went on, however, it seemed that students became less able to read required material in most classes.

I suspected that widespread television watching accounted for the lack of ability and interest in reading. Many children never developed a real love of reading. Reading began to be regarded as a purely practical skill, a tool to use in everyday life, a technique necessary to pass a test or to land a job. It was not the enriching experience, uplifting the heart and providing insights into life that I had known as a young person.

When I was growing up, we spent a good deal of our leisure time reading for pleasure. Weekly trips to the library provided us with fascinating stories of all times and places. My sister and I used to read for hours in all positions—sitting, lying right side up or upside down, even balancing ourselves on the branches of the large sycamore trees in front of the house in good weather. We preferred fiction, vicarious experiences of all kinds. In particular, we identified with characters of our same age and interests, so our reading levels grew as we did. At one stage we encountered the young sleuth Nancy Drew and can still recall a typical line from one of the mysteries: "Nancy skillfully backed the car out of the driveway." It annoyed us that Nancy always did everything skillfully. Our family's house had a narrow driveway. When my sister and I were old enough to drive, we frequently sheared off a few leaves of the neighbor's hydrangea bush when we backed out into the street. One day when I was the culprit, my sister came up to the car window and said, "Oh it's you—I thought the gardener was here." Neither of us could match Nancy Drew. We also listened to stories on the radio, such as the fairy tales on "Let's Pretend," a program sponsored by Cream of Wheat.

The theme song proclaimed that their cereal was "good for growing babies and grown-ups, too, to eat." The stories were delectable but the product only appealed to me when I was too sick to eat anything else.

I was an eighth grader when I first saw television. My family was invited across the street to view the Coronation of Queen Elizabeth. Shortly afterward, we acquired a small TV, which we put in my grandmother's bedroom. All six of us regularly joined her to watch "The Ed Sullivan Show," "The Hit Parade," and the few dramas offered. We brought in extra chairs for my parents. My two sisters, my brother and I either sat on her bed or on the floor. The shows were highly original, broadcast live, and rarely taped—regrettably. It would be wonderful to watch some of them again, such as the delightfully silly skits performed by Sid Caesar and Imogene Coca. Reading developed our imaginations, as did listening to stories and dramas on the radio. Many of the early television programs called for an intelligent, educated audience. Unfortunately, as time went on, much of the television fare demanded less and less from its viewers, eventually setting the stage for the entrance of the couch potato.

When I was puzzling over the high school reading problems I faced in teaching, I happened to read Walter Kerr's *Decline of Pleasure*. Kerr maintains that Americans have lost interest in the arts and, therefore, are incapable of experiencing the joy found in a type of recreation that truly refreshes us. He sees the arts as a major source of pleasure that we have been neglecting. Reading is one such pleasure. Kerr begins a discussion of reading development by referring to the time when comic books were widely read by most children. Educated adults tended to look upon comic books as inferior reading material, damaging to the child's educational progress. Kerr writes:

> Our instinct, on seeing a child curled up with a comic book, is
> to rip what is obviously crude and vulgar from his hands…. It
> does not occur to us to ask whether or not the child likes what
> he is reading, at this moment in time…confiscating the badly

drawn and garishly colored pages of pulp, we tell the child…
[to] go upstairs and read a 'good' book.

Kerr points out that this approach actually discourages the child from the enjoyment of reading. In fact, "the child is learning to define a 'good' book as something he doesn't like and…it may take some powerful persuasion a good many years later to break down his conviction." The best thing to do is to smile at the child and hand him twelve more comic books. When the child has read enough comic books, he or she will eventually tire of them and be ready for a higher level of reading. "The great danger of attempting to impose a higher taste upon a lower one at any time is the possibility of paralyzing both the higher and the lower responses," writes Kerr.

My brother and sisters and I read comic books voraciously, in addition to library books. In the closet, we had a cardboard box almost large enough to crawl into, filled with comics. Trading comic books was a regular social activity. When we visited my cousins' house, there was little initial conversation between us. We visitors plunked down on the couch with whatever comic book we spied that we hadn't read. One of my favorites was Superman, whose outfit inspired my Halloween costume early on. Another was Bucky Bug, a cute little "man ladybug" who lived in a mushroom house and had adventures with grasshoppers, honey bees, etc. Bucky's tale was always followed by a story about Mary Jane and Sniffles, a mouse. Mary Jane was able to shrink to a tiny size by eating magic cookies. She and Sniffles then set off together on exciting adventures. Being the same height, they wandered through forests of grass or explored cupboards and tabletops of the gigantic house. I preferred Bucky—Mary Jane was too nice.

Eventually a publisher provided Classics Comics, a comic book series of classic novels. The idea was intriguing, but I had read enough library books to suspect that *Man in the Iron Mask* and *Lorna Doone* in comic book form would fall far short of the actual book. What could the comic book hold in store except pictures and the plot? All the excitement of living the story along with the characters would be lost. There was more to a good book than the story line. Bucky Bug was fun, but wouldn't make the classics' list.

I began to realize that many of the teenagers I was teaching had never really gotten into a book. As time went on, I adopted the practice of asking them a little about themselves in an initial composition assignment. I included the question, "What books have you read in the last few years?" To my horror, I found that many of them had never read an entire novel. They had been studying novels as if they were scientific phenomena, using Cliffs Notes and notes from their teachers' lectures to answer test questions. Literature was becoming more like an archeological study—the experience of reading the book was no longer necessary.

A good work of literature, like any good work of art, has a life of its own. Most important in the study of literature is the students' responsive encounter with the work itself. St. Thomas Aquinas believed that there is no true knowledge without love. To develop a love of reading, one must experience the subtle seduction of being drawn into a work of literature, to feel with the hero or heroine, to struggle through conflicts that ultimately yield insights into one's own life. The way to be drawn in, as Kerr suggested, is through enjoyment. Since fewer students read for pleasure, classics that had been traditionally taught at the high school level gradually rose above the reading level of many students. *Great Expectations, MacBeth,* and *Huckleberry Finn* became works to know something about, rather than to know personally, like knowing facts about another person, instead of actually meeting him or her.

In an attempt to address the reading level problem, some teachers chose more recent novels and stories. Unfortunately many of these works were written by negative existentialists and expressed nihilistic, pessimistic views of life. Literature has a spiritual influence; these works did not give students a Christian worldview. As Madeline L'Engle writes in *Walking on Water*: "We don't want to feel less when we have finished a book; we want to feel that new possibilities of being have been opened to us. We don't want to close a book with a sense that life is totally unfair and that there is no light in the darkness; we want to feel that we have been given illumination."

Reading good works of literature has a transformative power, but requires true engagement and response from the reader, a wrestling with the work, a person-to-person encounter. If television was one of the culprits in the decline of reading, perhaps it was because television can be manipulative, and self-contained, requiring no response from the viewer. Robert Sardello has written, "Everything is provided with television: sound, image, character, plot. Television requires no inner work, and because no inner work is done, no transformation of the viewer can occur."

An educational journal of the time stated that, by the sixth grade, the reading level of the students in one classroom might vary from a third grade level to a senior high level. To combat the reading problem, a number of programs were initiated in both public and private schools. In two high schools where I taught, an hour a week was set aside for private reading. All business in the school stopped, and all teachers and students (sometimes even staff) spent the time reading a personally chosen book. In one school, administrators—who were supposed to be reading also—circulated to check on the carrying out of the program. An insecure member of the English Department in that school told me that he thought the program was really just an excuse for evaluators to catch him with his book down. A boy in one of my classes discovered some best-sellers and spent the time eagerly looking through the novel for spicy passages, which he held up to share with the boy behind him. It was not my favorite way of reading. It reminded me of trying to meditate with a chapel full of sisters all facing the same direction, except in this case, I had to face the students to be sure they kept looking at their books. I preferred to read and to meditate alone.

Meanwhile the emphasis on objective, factual, information affected all areas of study. It was important to know everything from the outside, as it were, defining and labeling reality, but ignoring the inner dimension. The curriculum seemed to be developed for the purpose of passing SAT tests and meeting other exterior norms of achievement. Pragmatism was rampant; practical skills were all-important in order to get a job. School philosophies spoke of the education of the whole person, but the detached objectivity valued in science and math was the sought-after attitude.

All in all, the emphasis in education was given to accumulating answers to pass tests, rather than exploring the great questions of life. Because of large class sizes, many teachers steered away from essay tests and even from including a few essay questions. Students' writing skills suffered from the combination of reading less and being asked to write infrequently. A college English teacher expressed her dismay in a professional journal. She described her frustration in trying to read compositions written by "aliens" who not only had few ideas, but no experience with the written word. I knew where she was coming from, but neither of us could identify the home planet of the aliens satisfactorily.

Some critics of the system compared the educational mode of the time to a filling station in which the teacher fills the students' minds with facts that are to be returned in an unaltered form on a test. Others used a banking analogy whereby the teacher deposits information into the student's account. Sadly, the deposit earns no interest over time, since it is soon withdrawn to pass a test. In the mid-1970s an article in *Media and Methods* satirized the process. Having read the piece, I took a large brown paper bag to class on which I had written, "THIS IS A TEST," following the model in the magazine. Circling the bag was a set of instructions in small print, which included the word "regurgitate." I placed the bag on my desk one morning and a bewildered bevy of sophomores stood around staring at it. I meant it as a joke, but it turned out to be a failed vocabulary test. The class was unacquainted with the "r" word, and no one ran to a dictionary for enlightenment.

The idea that regurgitated answers are the aim of education was also satirized in a science fiction story that I taught, entitled "The Sack." In that story, the answers are "in the bag." The Sack, a burlap bag resembling a sack of potatoes, is found on another planet. The Sack can not only talk, but can answer any question in the universe. The astronauts bring it back to Earth, causing a great power struggle—everyone wants to own it. Finally, after much of the world has been plunged into chaos, one character has the sense to ask the Sack the most important question: "Is it good for us to ask you questions?" The Sack renders its most important answer, "NO." It went on to explain that when humans are given answers without going through the process of finding them, they have missed the only important part of arriving at knowledge, which is the struggle itself.

Meanwhile, the administrators of high schools had to face the challenge of turning out educated students. The principal of one of the schools decided to require daily, detailed lesson plans from all teachers. I was the English Department chair and realized that we English teachers were already burdened with paper work. In fact, we were carrying the burden of being responsible for correct writing for practically the whole school, with little support from members of the other departments. As long as their students learned the given material, many teachers in the other departments didn't feel it was their job to demand acceptable writing from their students, blaming shabby work in the assignments turned in to them on our department. Programs like "Writing Across the Curriculum" hadn't occurred to anyone at the time.

After I read the lesson plan directive from the principal's office, I developed a severe cold. Coughing my way into the early hours of the morning, I realized that I was really just plain angry and probably had succumbed to a cold germ by exhausting my energy to repress my feelings. I decided to write the principal a letter expressing my thoughts and feelings. I judged it to be a well-written letter, stating my points clearly. However, I did use one word of strong language in it, namely the phrase "hog wash." I sent the letter immediately and later met with the principal after I recovered.

Whether in response to my strong language or to my disagreement with his policy, he definitely had a strong reaction. He was shocked. Colorful language was not as acceptable as educational jargon was, and sisters were supposed to be obedient. He told me that he could hardly believe that an experienced teacher and a religious would express such views. I wasn't sure at the time if I should have spoken up at all, or if I should have done so long ago. I had suggested at the end of the letter that he ask any experienced high school or college teacher not under his jurisdiction what he or she thought of his policy. I myself asked an experienced sister principal what she thought and she said, "I'm just glad if the teachers are all in their classrooms." In any case, I packed my bags again at the end of that year—this time voluntarily.

Years later I had a similar experience at another school. By this time computer skills were being taught, and computers were used extensively in the school offices. The principal had thought up a foolproof scheme for dealing with teacher absences and inadequate substitution plans. He directed all of the teachers to put their entire semester lesson plans on computer discs, including the pages to be read, and the work to be done. In the event of a teacher's absence, the office staff could just pop the disc into the computer and hand the substitute a complete lesson for the class. The principal stated that he wanted the school to "run just as smoothly as Boys' Market." He was all for simplification. When it was reported to him that students had been dropping food and trash near the lunch benches, he had the benches removed. I thought at the time that he might have done better to have had the students removed.

Much earlier I had written a satirical piece about how to address the problem of insufficient teachers' salaries. Like the removal of lunch benches, it was also a simple plan. The students could stay at home and the teachers could then live in the school building and conduct correspondence courses. That way the teachers could be saved the cost of renting an apartment, and also be spared the irritation of the students' actual presence. I would have shared the satire with that principal, but I wasn't sure that his sense of humor was up to it.

Fortunately I met many men and women faculty members who did value humor. We supported each other through the rigors of teaching high school by sharing our frustrations and educational theories, but humor helped the most. In one of the schools, black was one of the two official school colors. Black balloons were rarely seen in those days. I saw one for the first time at a rally. A history teacher who became a friend of mine stared at it. He turned to me and said, "It makes you think that a clown died somewhere, doesn't it?" To encourage us in our teaching efforts, one administrator gave out "Teacher of the Week" awards. An English teacher who was chosen for a particular week opened his blinds to see a poster of an ineffectual-looking teacher above the caption "Teacher of the Weak." I encountered another instance of imaginative humor when I phoned a fellow English teacher and on his answering machine was the message, "We can't come to the phone right now, but leave your name and number, and mention one embarrassing incident from your childhood and we will return your call."

Of course, we had other duties than teaching, such as chaperoning dances. I finally invested in a pair of ear plugs when the popular music began to sound like artillery barrages. After one of the loudest live bands came to the end of a number, a few faculty members near me applauded loudly. When I directed a mystified gaze in their direction, one winked, saying, "We're clapping because it stopped." Continuous chaperoning went on during the day at coed schools. A woman teacher who had observed and discouraged two freshmen kissing in the hall remarked to me, "How would you like to kiss someone with junk food in their braces before eight o'clock in the morning?" After school I walked by a pair who were leaning against each other as if they were disabled. I asked if they were waiting for a ride. When they said yes, I suggested that they wait a little farther apart. They reluctantly complied.

Five

Time Out for Answers

Having become English department chair in several schools, I was able to design and teach classes that I really enjoyed. One was an Advanced Placement English class. I hadn't believed it to be in the students' best interests to substitute credit from a high school class for college units, thereby skipping more needed study in literature and writing. But when the school decided to offer the class, I chose literature that I valued to share with the class. One year the class was filled with lively, delightful students who appreciated depth, humor and even some of my own poetry. After we had finished the major work of the course and the A.P. test was over, we took a day off from the regular work. One of the scientifically minded boys taught the class the aerodynamics involved in creating a streamlined paper airplane. As a break from having confronted major challenges on paper in the form of reading and writing, we sailed sheets of wordless, airborne paper through the room.

Most high schools gave yearly musicals, so I was able to keep playing the violin by helping out in small orchestral groups. Usually the orchestra consisted of a handful of players who sat in a dark corner, neither able to see the stage, nor to be seen themselves. But it was a fine experience—sound only! I played for "Fiddler on the Roof" in two schools and dressed up like a Russian peasant in one play, standing behind the curtain to give a silhouette effect of playing on the roof. It reminded me of a time when I was younger and had wanted to climb up onto the roof and play a few notes just to be able to say that I had fiddled on a roof.

In the parishes and schools of the 1970s, patriarchal administrations had been long established. It took a good number of years for the innovations of Vatican II to be implemented as far as lay leadership was concerned. Unfortunately, because of the dualistic view of authority—the clergy having all the authority, the lay people next to none—the issue of adequate salaries for lay teachers in the schools was not addressed in an amicable, free-flowing discussion. The lay teachers finally resorted to a strike in the diocesan schools. Many administrators saw it as an adolescent rebellion, and perhaps it was, in the sense that adult "children" had not been consulted as equals in ministry. The strike caused divisions between lay and religious friends alike. I was asked to substitute indefinitely for a few striking teachers, but had mixed feelings about splitting a Christian community over something that appeared to be a just cause.

By the time of my Silver Jubilee in 1982, I had made many friends—religious, faculty members, and a few special students with whom I still communicate. The community I lived with hosted a fine celebration for my family and friends. My father, the gourmet cook, was persuaded to cook orange crêpes for a breakfast following Mass in our chapel. A white dove appeared from nowhere and stayed in the garden for about nine days, letting me feed it. It must have been someone's escaped pet, but seemed to have arrived especially for the occasion. Following the Mass for my jubilee group at our motherhouse, we exited to the song, "Here I am, Lord...Is it I, Lord?...I will go Lord, if you lead me." As I walked out, having been reunited with my original entrance group for a few days, I wondered where I would be led next.

While I was wading unknowingly into the waters of midlife, religious life was working through a period similar to that of adolescence. When I had entered, religious life functioned much like a parent/child relationship. Religious obedience meant that the "subjects" followed the orders of the "superiors." A sister friend told me that a provincial superior had once phoned her to say, "I hear you've been thinking—I want you to stop." At first I thought she was joking. A joke had circulated earlier about a priest coming to say Mass at a novitiate house. When a young sister opened the door he said, "Isn't it a nice day, sister?" To which the sister replied, "Excuse me, Father—I'll have to ask Mother Superior." But my friend's experience was real.

The adolescent aspect in religious life had to do with delayed stages in human development. Many sisters, brothers, and priests had entered religious life only a few months after graduating from high school. The major developmental task of adolescence is to establish an identity. Peer groups usually provide support for teenagers during the process of necessary separation from their parents. Although this time is painful for parents, their children are just following a natural, but unconscious path toward growth. I once read that adolescents think unconsciously.

On tedious teaching days in high school, I worked up a little adrenaline by frightening myself with the idea. Passing through crowds of large creatures between classes, I repeated to myself, "They're all thinking unconsciously—watch your step!" I felt it was a step up from my younger days when I had taken my sister into a corner to elicit a few screams by showing her the witch in the Snow White book. Having repented of the actions of those days—at least partially—I found providing myself with a little scare on dull days to be helpful.

Fortunately, by the time they were seniors, high school students had grown to some degree out of complete peer identification. They usually decided on a particular field of study or line of work to pursue after graduation. However, many who had entered religious life immediately after high school were still in the process of forming a personal identity. Erik Erikson describes an adolescent as "a combination of vulnerability and strength" who "can put an enormous amount of energy and loyalty at the disposal of any convincing system." He or she is willing to conform for the sake of a feeling of belonging. Becoming a member of a religious congregation certainly provided a sense of group identity.

With the new freedoms resulting from the directives of Vatican II, conformity decreased. Religious had the opportunity for more personal choices in ministry, study programs, retreats, schedules, and living situations. When I was a young sister, we were required to have a sister companion to go anywhere outside the convent grounds, and to obtain a special permission from the provincial superior to stay overnight, even in another convent. The rules were clear and rigid. When the tight structure began to give way to more flexibility, the freedom involved raised questions of identity, which some of us had not faced before. "Keep the Rule, and the Rule will keep you," had been the maxim that had relegated our decision making to a compliance with the stated regulations. Following the collective pattern had supplied many of us with a ready-made identity.

Erikson also states that "the more highly structured a culture is, the less likely that there will be an overt conflict of identity, while the less structure there is in a free society, the greater will be the conflict." It is true that a few of the young people who entered religious life at the time I did had either completed college or had worked for a few years. These may have developed a greater sense of identity than those entering directly from high school. However, as Erikson goes on to say, "Even though one has resolved his [or her] identity crisis, later changes in life can precipitate a renewal of crisis." Thus the changes in religious life posed a problem for all of us to some degree.

In Erikson's scheme of human development, the stage following the establishing of an identity is the challenge of forming intimate personal relationships with others, which is ordinarily a preparation for marriage and family life. For the large numbers who entered religious life when I did, intimacy was discouraged—even friendships within our own communities. Heterosexual friendships were rare. Many religious and priests had never experienced the intimacy of an adult friendship with anyone. To compound the problem, little education was provided for religious concerning the realities of human sexuality in the context of celibate living.

In a series of tapes entitled "Celibacy and Sexuality," Sr. Barbara Becnel remarks, "It isn't that what we were taught was wrong. It's that we weren't taught anything about how to love." However, she quotes a statement from the spiritual writer, Rodriguez, that tends to belie her first statement: "It was by love that sin entered the world." When I entered, we were all given large or small doses of Rodriguez's spirituality. We were taught that feelings don't count, but the truth is that if feelings are simply repressed, they descend to a subconscious level, having the potential to surface and sabotage us later in life.

In any case, the summer schools, conventions, workshops and freedom of mobility in general for men and women religious provided opportunities for personal relationships to develop. People fell in love, formed close friendships and, at the least, began to be more aware of the need to bond intimately with others. Since the new freedom triggered identity problems, there was a great deal of confusion and anxiety involved. Many left religious life, some to marry, others to live a single life. Some left because of the hardships caused them by what they saw as an oppressive system, some for personal needs and reevaluation. I had begun to read a little in the Jungian field of psychology and suspected that there might be a good deal of unconscious behavior going on.

Although falling in love brings with it delightful feelings, it is a temporary state, which can lead to either a deeper, more mature love or to a regressive search for the initial delights of the experience. I had read Martin D'Arcy's *The Mind and Heart of Love* in which the Jesuit author proposed that "standing in love" was superior to "falling in love." The latter stage, if not undergone and outgrown, could lead to divorce, despair and even suicide, as it did in *Romeo and Juliet*. D'Arcy's main example was that of Tristan and Isolde, another falling-in-love that ended in death.

I had the unexpected pleasure of meeting Martin D'Arcy in person some years after I had read his book. I saw him in the pew in front of me at a Holy Week service at Loyola Marymount University. He was then a slight, elderly man. The afternoon sun seemed to stream directly through his generous ears, illuminating tufts of protruding gray hair. A teacher friend of mine invited him to her apartment, where a number of our friends gathered. D'Arcy sipped a Manhattan as he spoke of a personal encounter with C. S. Lewis. "He didn't look the part," said D'Arcy. "He looked more like a butcher—a large bald man with a ruddy face." A writer's appearance certainly doesn't have to match his or her subject, I thought, gazing at D'Arcy. Who would suspect this frail wisp of a man to have written a profound book about passion and the nature of love?

Meanwhile, midlife caught up with me. "As we grow older/The world becomes stranger, the pattern more complicated," writes T. S. Eliot. Looking back, the experience reminds me of a scene from the film based on *The Phantom Tollbooth*. The heroes have completed the arduous journey to find the Castle in the Air, to rescue the Princesses of Rhyme and Reason, and to return them to the Kingdom of Wisdom in order to restore sanity to the land. Having passed through the Mountains of Ignorance, they finally see the castle. "There it is! We're home free! No more problems! Clear sailing!" they shout. Meanwhile, directly behind them, the demons of the mountains move silently toward them.

A few years later I read *Celebrate Midlife*, in which the authors compare the onset of midlife to a sudden realization that the ladder you've been climbing all these years is leaning up against the wrong roof. James Finley likened the midlife experience to that of a person who has climbed to the top of a hill, only to see "where it's all going from here." At this stage he said, "You begin to sense a downhill direction, which suggests that your wagon isn't hitched to a star, but to a hole in the ground." Quite a grounding thought. Realizing that I had developed a case of ministry burnout, I requested and was granted a sabbatical year.

I realized that I had been putting more effort into teaching, with what appeared to be fewer results. The break up of a friendship and several physical problems added to my distress, bringing me to realize that I needed time out.

I signed up for a spiritual development program that offered updating in theology, enrichment classes, communal interacting, and several retreats during the year. Once a week the group met for Mass followed by dinner in a house near Loyola Marymount, the university sponsoring the program. Before our first Mass, we were to write down a prayer asking God for what we thought we each needed from the program that year. We then placed the papers on the altar. I wrote, "I don't know. I'm tired. You figure it out." Before folding up the paper, I showed it to a sister next to me who said, "You're bad!" However, by that time I was convinced that one didn't have to be polite when praying—thank God.

During that year, I had time to recover physically and emotionally and continue the private study of human development that I had begun. I attended a workshop given by James Gill, S.J., a psychiatrist, who emphasized how important it is for clergy and religious to form real friendships with others and to develop good relationships with those to whom they minister, indicating that establishing these bonds takes time. He suggested that the authorities responsible should not "just shoot religious or priests from one place to another." His idea was that frequent moves diminish the quality of our ministry because if we don't work on being integral ourselves, we can't help others. Relocating too frequently to put down roots for any length of time results in fragmentation and precludes opportunities for necessary reflection and development.

With so many leaving religious life and marrying, the important question for those of us who still felt called to religious life was "How do we work on being integral?" The fact that a good number of the attempted relationships didn't last may bear out Erikson's comments, "Many young people marry in order to find their identity in and through another person, but this is difficult where the very choice of partner was made to resolve a severe unconscious conflict." To be really intimate, a stable identity must at least be in process. From his insights I gathered that a firm identity is also a prerequisite for making a commitment to God in religious life.

In high school I had an excellent Latin teacher who gave me the impression that she had actually lived during the time period of the ancient texts we were deciphering. An elderly sister in full habit, she introduced one of the readings to us by saying that the man and woman in the selection "were quite good friends—in fact, they were engaged to be married." My friends and I found this statement deliciously humorous, a nice bit to take home to share. Our humor was based on the assumption that the relationships of friendship and of marriage were entirely different in nature. As time went on I observed that not all marriages included real friendship and that true friendships did not require overt physical expression. Somewhere along the line, the words "love" and "sex" or "relationship" and "sex" began to be used interchangeably—more confusion.

During that sabbatical year I explored the problem further. St. John wrote, "God is love, and he who abides in love abides in God, and God abides in him." Robert Johnson notes that whereas other languages have terms for different kinds of love, we have only one word to cover every kind. Although this limitation might be considered a disadvantage, perhaps the use of only one word expresses the idea that love takes different forms, but has only one nature. C. S. Lewis in *The Four Loves* attempts to classify love in four different ways: *storge* (affection), *filia* (friendship), *eros* (romance), and *agape* (unconditional love for all).

I began to wonder why the term "love" seemed to be used more infrequently, being replaced by "relationship." According to the dictionary, relationship has a number of denotations. It can mean "the relationship between variables," "kinship" or "a romantic or passionate attachment." The ambiguity inherent in any relationship calls to mind a story told to me by a colorful substitute teacher. He provided the faculty with a constant stream of Irish stories. One concerned a man who was driving down an Irish lane, accompanied by an incurably talkative wife. When the man stopped at a crossroads, a younger man ran up breathlessly to tell him, "Your wife fell out of the car a few minutes ago." The husband, with a look of relief, replied, "Thank God! I thought I was going deaf!"

A contrast to the relationship described in the satirical Irish joke is the intimacy shown between two war comrades in *All Quiet on the Western Front*. Having carried his wounded friend Kat out of the line of fire, Paul, the young hero of the novel, is grief-stricken when he realizes that Kat has died on the way to the dressing station. The orderly asks Paul if he wants Kat's wallet and belongings. Paul is in shock and only nods. The orderly is mystified by the intensity of the emotion gripping Paul and asks if the two soldiers are related. Paul manages to mutter, "No, we are not related. No, we are not related." His reply is a poignant contradiction to his own feelings and to the intimacy they had shared in undergoing the horrors of war. "Do I walk? Have I feet still?…All is as usual. Only the militiaman Stanislaus Katczinsky has died," Paul thinks to himself. Paul and Kat were intimate friends, bonded by deep feelings, but their friendship was not romantic.

Helen Luke, in several of her essays, gives some valuable insights into romantic love: "A boy or girl, if he or she is to plunge into life in any real way, *must* fall in love with someone or something. This does not refer, of course, to the easy, promiscuous, so-called 'falling in love' which is mere appetite, but to the true romantic love of which Charles Williams has so beautifully written. This love is a glimpse of the ultimate glory, which cannot last in that form but is nonetheless valid and beautiful." However, she adds, "The romantic projection, so essential to youth, is extremely destructive in maturity." A romantic projection can serve as an initial "hook" to attract people to each other, but it is a passing stage. The search to recapture a romantic state after it has passed is a refusal to move toward a deeper, more realistic type of love. Luke writes, "Demanding…that it be returned to us exactly as it was, without any effort to discover the meaning of the experience," ends in frustration and prevents growth toward maturity. Even if we think we have restored the status quo, it will pass away again, endlessly repeating the pattern until we make the effort to understand.

In spite of the problems of projection, intimacy is a necessary developmental stage in everyone's life if one is to mature. According to Erikson, the stages of generativity (valuable contributions to the next generation) and wisdom (integrated wholeness through experience) are dependent on having experienced intimacy in some form. Richard Rohr has stated that "Intimacy has to be happening somewhere" if a true Christian community is to exist. Charles Williams has written, "Do we believe in the Incarnation of Love in Christ? Then our job is to know and to welcome him, and in him, all the lesser incarnations of love that we can find, whatever form they take."

Because of the prohibitions against intimacy, it seemed that some religious settled for a brand of superficial chumminess. Von Hildebrand writes that this type of relating is not consistent with the profound goals of religious life—only deep friendships are really appropriate. In a recent book, Barbara Fiand refers to the attempts of religious to relate to each other that produce a false closeness, which encourages them to "talk too long…laugh too loudly…or agree too soon" with one another's opinions. She describes intimacy as a reality that "allows for space to grow, for littleness and vulnerability and honesty." True intimacy results in authentic friendship.

Interestingly, I found that the word "relationship" as a synonym for "love" is of fairly recent origin. Shakespeare never uses it, although he frequently uses the word "love" in a variety of contexts. John O'Donohue deals with the idea of "soul-love" in *Anam Cara*. The title of his book is a Gaelic phrase that means "soul friend." He writes that the word "relationship" has become "an empty center around which our lonely hunger forges for warmth and belonging. Much of the public language of intimacy is hollow and its incessant repetition only betrays the complete absence of intimacy. Real intimacy is a sacred experience...of the soul, and the soul is reserved."

Given that intimacy is a necessary developmental experience, one's attitude toward the risks involved may differ. Because intimacy was discouraged in the religious life of the past, many people simply avoided it. Some were afraid of the pain or sacrifice entailed. Charles Williams writes, "To be or to desire to be, free from being hurt by others, is to be, or to desire to be, free from the co-inherence of all human souls, which it was the express intention of Christ to redeem." There is no real love without some pain involved.

On the other hand, there is in our time a tendency to idolize intimacy, to deify love. James Hollis in his introduction to *The Eden Project* states that he wrote the book to expose some "generalized fantasies about relationships that permeate our culture." In addition to addressing the problem of people's desires to be saved or rescued by means of relationships, he suggests that romantic love has even taken the place of institutionalized religion as "the greatest motive, power and influence in our lives." He even proposes that "the search for love has replaced the search for God. Shocking thought? Untrue? Simply surf the stations on the radio." Here he refers to music that expresses the longing to find and merge with the perfect magical other.

The painful truth about romantic projections is that they do not last. In the aftermath of disillusion we tend to blame the other. But perhaps Pogo, the satirical comic book possum, comes nearer the truth by saying, "We have met the Enemy and he is us." Hollis offers a similar insight, "Only when one has suffered the collapse of projections onto the Other, or tracked symptomology to its lair, may one begin to realize that the enemy is within." In other words, we project onto others the undeveloped or repressed parts of ourselves—either blaming others or idolizing them.

Continued reading in the Jungian field of psychology had given me a better understanding of Jung's theory of the development of the psyche.

The ego is the conscious personality that we develop over the years in order to meet the standards and ideals of our parents, of society, of our particular religion, etc. Those qualities we don't develop are potentialities that fall into the shadow. Edward C. Whitmont has defined "shadow" as "that part of the personality which has been repressed for the sake of the ego ideal." These underdeveloped parts, both positive and negative, can be projected, as in romantic projection. We then either idealize or scapegoat the other. Since the projections are unconscious, we usually need a knock on the head of some kind to begin to see others as they truly are. Close relationships usually provide the disturbing knock. Most of us are tempted at this point to plead, "*Please*—Don't confuse me with the facts."

Robert Bly compares our situation to that of a person who has stuffed his or her unacceptable qualities into a large bag over the years, eventually closing the bag and forgetting about the contents. Bly writes, "We spend our life until we're twenty deciding what parts of ourself to put into the bag, and we spend the rest of our lives trying to get them out again." If we haven't peeked into the bag by midlife, opening it can precipitate a crisis. At this time we need to start looking into the bag to sort things out, to claim and befriend our rejected qualities. Otherwise they can become demons, in the sense that they begin to work against us.

It has been said that the first half of life is a trial run for the second half. Jung wrote, "Whoever carries into the afternoon the law of the morning…must pay for doing so with damage to his [her] soul." When the pattern of life we have established by midlife no longer works for us, we need to become aware of our forgotten potentialities that have been banished into the bag of our personal unconscious, lest we be sabotaged by them. If we refuse this task, we risk falling into depression, stagnation, physical illness, or another crisis of some kind. We must go at least semi-willingly or we will be pulled in that direction, either kicking and screaming, or merely dragging our heels, thus making the transition more difficult.

Holding on to our ego stance and identity at midlife leads to egocentricity. Letting go enough to explore other aspects of ourselves leads to wholeness. Hopefully, this psychological work will be blessed with the grace to usher our egocentric ego gently off center stage, giving way to the realization that the Spirit dwells within. Therefore St. Paul writes, "I live now, not I, but Christ lives within me." Perhaps Jesus' words to Peter symbolize the necessary relinquishment of egocentricity. "Truly, I say to you, when you were young, you girded yourself and walked where you would; but when you are old, you will stretch out your hands, and another will gird you and carry you where you do not wish to go." The gospel writer comments that Jesus said this, "to show by what death he was to glorify God." But the passage might be taken on another level and applied to the turnabout of control found in the conversion experience of midlife.

Here another example from Pogo comes to mind. Pogo lives in the Okefenokee Swamp with his friends: Albert, the alligator; Churchy La Femme, the turtle; Howland Owl, and others. They usually wander through the swamp talking their way into confusing situations. In one adventure, through a misinterpretation of words, the owl believes that he is the rightful king of the swamp. Most of the main characters accept the illusion, suddenly seeing him as worthy of their loyalty and service. The owl king decides to bestow visits on his subjects throughout the swamp. He and his courtiers mount a large cow that has been innocently munching nearby and gallop through the swamp. The king shouts, "Joy subjects, Joy!" as they ride right over the picnic of a family of little animals on the ground. The owl's illusion is similar to that of the vain, egocentric ruler in "The Emperor's New Clothes." But at least no one gets hurt in that tale. However, both kings suffer from egotistical, inflated self-perceptions, deceiving both themselves and their willing subjects.

The main difficulty of this egocentric state is that, as Jung has stated, any triumph of the greater Self is a defeat for the ego. The ego has become the ruler of the psyche at this point and resists the suffering involved in the transformation to a broader base of consciousness. The ego "has its little ways," as does King John in A. A. Milne's Christmas poem. To relinquish control to a higher Self feels like death to the ego, and so it is, in the sense that a former stage must be let go of in moving to another level. However, people who refuse the challenge, remaining in a stage of arrested development, may be putting themselves at risk. My father once said that eggs faint just before they're cracked, to save themselves from trauma. After cracking them, we can feel free to use them in omelets or soufflés without hurting their feelings. People who resist giving up ego control sometimes are cracked by inner or outer events—a physical breakdown, an accident, a tragedy—without having the eggs' option of fainting first. Life seems to provide situations beyond our control to push us toward wholeness.

The harder one tries to hold on to the ego ideal at midlife, the harder it is to maintain. Robert Johnson has said, "For every three steps I take, I slip back two, but it's all right because I was going the wrong way in the first place." David Richo refers to an Egyptian word for "death" that is synonymous with "holding on." To express the idea that a person has died, the words "he died" literally mean "he held on" in that language. The expression implies that the person in question became stiff and lifeless. Clinging to an egocentric state, suggests Richo, produces a rigid, inflexible personality, incapable of growth.

The reading and reflecting I had done during the sabbatical year suggested to me the importance of getting to know oneself well. The year passed all too soon, but it had provided me with enriching experiences in addition to a needed rest. In addition to the spiritual development program, I had also audited classes in theater, philosophy, mythology, and chamber music. The insights I gained during the sabbatical year proved to be valuable future resources.

I returned to teaching English for the next thirteen years—seven of them in two more high schools and the next six at the college level. The more significant experiences during those years, however, were those of inner exploration and psychological work. One of the tools that I found most helpful was the Myers-Briggs Type Indicator. I had resisted taking it for a number of years because it seemed to be just a fad. I thought of it as a sort of alphabet soup parlor game. People were asking each other, "Are you an "N" or an "S?" Others were declaring, "I'm an "F," but he's a "T." Finally one of my high school principals arranged a session for the faculty. After learning something about it—and about myself—I began to see that it made sense. The concept is based on Jungian psychology, just a small but significant part of the vast subject. There are magazines, tapes, books, and associations exploring further and further into the topic. Unfortunately, like much current learning, many people took only one workshop about it, took notes, and then had fun identifying and labeling people before filing the notes away and turning to another interest.

The Myers-Briggs literature indicated that there might be a timeline for type development. Although there is evidence of type identification soon after birth, one theory states that it is clearly observable beginning at age six. Up to that age children identify mainly with the world of the family. I remember a woman who came to visit my mother when I was very young. As she was leaving, she said to me in a meaningful way, "My name is Mona, too." She seemed to expect a response from me, but I couldn't imagine why she thought the fact would be of the least significance to me. I was the only Mona in my world; she was someone who lived outside the screen door through which she was speaking, and who would, hopefully, go away soon. In a small child's world of the family, the parents seem magical and godlike. My father, for example, could magically produce candy. My mother sat in the front room with my sister and brother and me. The kitchen door always had to be closed while my father made candy. Loud sounds of metal pots and pans colliding issued from behind the door for a couple of minutes. Then my father emerged, bearing the newly created candies, nicely wrapped in cellophane and mounted on sticks for convenience. What wizardry!

The Myers-Briggs indicator measures four "functions." We all use these behaviors in some way, but we prefer one to the rest. This function is called "dominant." The others follow in degree of development through our natural inclinations. I tested out as a dominant "intuitive," an intuitive being a person who perceives possibilities through imagination and hunches as opposed to a dominant "sensate," who observes the world of practical reality through the five senses. According to the theory, we develop our dominant function from the age of six to about the age of twelve.

Dwelling on the imaginative possibilities (and even impossibilities) was definitely part of my early life. I remember entertaining myself by sitting next to a window imagining tiny figures of people on the sill who looked upon me as God. I tried to be kind and helpful to them. I knew they might be frightened by my size, so I calmed them down by talking to them. Sometimes we changed places and I became tiny, able to walk on the sill and talk to one of them who had become gigantic. In the garden I saw faces in the pansies and wondered what they might say if they spoke a few words. When Sunday rides into the foothills were a bit dull, I kept hoping that Mickey Mouse would jump out from behind a rock or a little hill to brighten up the landscape. At seven, I could count on my fingers to seven—it seemed quite symbolic at the time. Were mathematical skills and age connected? Would I have to wait another year to be able to count to eight?

My reading preferences also revealed an imaginative bent—I loved fairy tales. One book from the library showed a huge orange on a tree, surrounded by fairies who drank from the "sun fruit" by using long straws. A tale about a brown Easter rabbit who wore a pair of golden shoes is still in my head. Once I nearly caused my mother a car accident when I was reading a Babar book in the back seat. I came to the part where Cornelius, the oldest elephant, ate too much salt, turned green, and died. I let out a series of screams, at which my mother pulled over to see what had happened and then spent some time calming me down. The first movie I saw was "Snow White." I can still remember the magic of the sparkling gems in the Seven Dwarves' dark mine.

Carrying imagination into the drama field, I decided to dress up like a man, using some old clothing of my father's. I rang the front door bell and introduced myself as "Mr. Appooshian." We had a number of Armenian neighbors, so I thought it was a good disguise. I pretended to be new in the neighborhood and asked to be shown around the house. My brother recalled this event as "the time when Mona thought she was Mr. Appooshian."

The concentration given to developing a dominant function brings with it two possible extremes. One is overusing it to one's detriment. The anticipation of Christmas almost did me in with imaginative possibilities. Many times I was sick from nervous excitement on the day itself. One Christmas Eve I had trouble sleeping. My mother stayed with me part of the night, trying to calm me down, hinting that Santa might not come at all if I didn't go to sleep.

The other liability resulting from the development of an intuitive, imaginative approach to life is the tendency to neglect the physical realities in front of one's nose. The consequences can be painful, as were those of two early incidents I remember. During a summer vacation in the mountains, I ran right through a pile of ashes still hot underneath from a day-old bonfire and burned the soul of my foot badly. On another outing, a family picnic in the foothills, I raced down a hill, not seeing a clothesline in back of a rural house. The line caught me under the chin. I dropped on the ground, unable to see for a number of hours. The picnic was disrupted to take me back to town, blind and muddy after having fallen from the clothesline into the spring weeds.

The type development theory holds that we turn to a second function from about thirteen to twenty years old. I tested out as a "feeling" type as opposed to a "thinking" type. The "F" bases decisions on personal, subjective values. Sensitivity to people's feelings is important to this type. One of the drawbacks of the feeling type, who presents a friendly face to the world, is a growing inability to say "no," not wanting to hurt anyone. In my freshman year of high school I met an overweight, non-stop talker who asked me to go to a movie with her on the weekend. I didn't want to go with her, but said I would. For days I dreaded the event. When the day finally came, I suffered through the bus trip, pretending to be interested in her monologue on the way there and back. Then I spent several days kicking myself for having gone. But I didn't seem to be able to refuse her. I made the same mistake when a short boy with a rickety car asked me out on a date in my junior year. We went to an outdoor dance near the river at a place where the band played a type of country music that I hated. Again, I hadn't wanted to go, but couldn't say no.

Following my first year of college when I worked at a restaurant in Yosemite, a young man came in with some of his family. I served him an extra large plate of spaghetti. He happened to be from my parish in Fresno, and we went on several dates when I returned. I accepted his invitation of a fourth date, but my girlfriends were doing something I found more interesting that same evening. Not being able to bring myself to phone him and be honest, I just left the house before the time he was to arrive. He was a nice person, and it was a mean trick. I later apologized, but the fact that I had resorted to such an underhanded deception to avoid confrontation shocked me into self-scrutiny. What was it within me that had such difficulty saying no to people, or even disagreeing with them? Did I resemble Polonius in the scene from *Hamlet* in which he readily agrees with anything Hamlet suggests about the shape of a certain cloud?

Hamlet: Do you see yonder cloud that's almost in the shape of a camel?

Polonius: By the mass, and it is like a camel indeed.

Hamlet: Methinks it is like a weasel.

Polonius It is backed like a weasel.

Hamlet: Or like a whale.

Polonius: Very like a whale.

I thought of the girls at my high school teasing a new girl who wanted to be accepted into their group. They said things like, "Look at that sweater—isn't it beautiful?" After the girl answered "yes," they went on to suggest that the sweater was really almost puce—an ugly color, or that it made the wearer look fat, etc. The victim kept agreeing with them in order to please. Her situation was the typical plight of the "F" type, whose perennial temptation is to try too hard to please others for the sake of harmony.

We usually develop a third function from ages twenty-one to forty. For me, the third preference is the thinking function designated as "T." People using this preference make judgments according to logic and impersonal objective standards. During my twenties I began to choose different reading material. Rather than concentrating on fiction, I read works of philosophy, theology, and spirituality, as well. It was then that I began keeping notebooks of significant quotations, reviewing them regularly to compare with what I was currently reading. This shift probably accounts for my eventual interest in objective personality studies like the Myers-Briggs.

It was no surprise that I tested out as an introvert, as opposed to an outgoing extravert. Although I, like other teenagers, probably lived through the period unconsciously, I do admit to showing a friendly, adaptive face to the world, while thinking my own thoughts. I was usually quiet and cooperative in my classes. One notable exception is the time that I built a dummy student out of an old school sweater in the back of my chemistry class. The sister teaching us became so absorbed in her lecture that she didn't concentrate on the back of the room. My lack of interest in objective facts probably drove me to it. When I started rolling Tootsie Rolls back and forth on a yardstick between myself and the dummy, the movement derailed her train of thought, and her gaze swept the back row. It was the only time I stayed after school involuntarily.

Another personality tool that I found to be valuable was the Enneagram. Again I hesitated to take an interest because of the popularity of the topic. It was the latest thing and much bandied about in small talk. Those who had taken workshops or read books about the nine Enneagram types seemed to think they "had everyone's number" and interpreted others' behavior accordingly: "Well, she must be a two—she's more eager to serve me a cup of coffee than I am to have one." Bonds formed between people having the same number: "Oh you're a seven? So am I. Let's find a happy hour and talk." Eventually I became curious and went to a weekend workshop on the topic. There was no test to take at the end; one had to take some time in self-reflection and observation in order to recognize in oneself a tendency that fit one of the nine patterns. The understanding was, as with the Myers-Briggs, that we all have some of the characteristics of all of the types, but prefer and develop a particular one.

The description of the number five seemed to fit me the best—that of a curious, mentally alert information gatherer who tries to avoid emptiness within. The five is primarily an observer with a need to perceive and interpret outer realities and to ask and answer the question, "What's it all about?" The five spends much time engrossed in reading and speculation. Had I any doubts about my Enneagram type, I had only to look at the pig bookends given to me by a friend. They could hold only a fraction of the number of books I always had on hand. Most were on shelves, but some always covered parts of the floor, the desk, almost any available surface. The implication of the gift was that I was a "book pig," and I couldn't deny it. In addition to the books were notebooks that I had been keeping since before I was sent out to teach. I only copied down a few pithy sentences from each book, but the notebooks began to pile up. In one I had written Emerson's statement, "Try to be one of those on whom nothing is lost." At this point in life I was beginning to have trouble finding some of the things that I hadn't wanted to lose.

The Enneagram theory ascribes a certain animal to each type as a symbol. One animal associated with the five is the owl, who watches wide-eyed from the darkness of a tree branch, but is itself hard to locate in the night. Owls have always fascinated me. I have owned a number of little art pieces shaped like owls. A friend of mine made an "owl suit" for me that I have worn to a number of Halloween gatherings. The five's defense tactic is withdrawal from whatever involvement seems either threatening or boring. An article by Loretta Brady quoted in an issue of "Enneagram Monthly," states "[fives] have a way of looking like they are still in the room and still in the conversation while actually they have left. Their emotions are drawn away to a safe hiding place. And their minds are in another world of observation and reflection. Only their bodies are present, but they show little movement or emotional display."

I can recall conversations at the family table when the topic hadn't interested me. I had tuned in occasionally to avoid suspicion, but had wandered off somewhere else mentally. The embarrassing result was not being able to recall what had been said when a family member referred back to some item under discussion. Of course, I carried the trait into convent life. School and community meetings provided opportunities for slipping out my mental back door. Sometimes I would vary the escape by sketching the people in the room—their heads, or just feet or glasses. Another alternative was to write silly notes to myself, sometimes passing them to others who looked as if they also were seeking an escape. A temptation for fives is to become recluses, living in isolation, like owls alone in the forest. Several factors had saved me from this pitfall. Not only did my extraverted feeling function draw me to people, but community life and teaching provided me with what I felt was more than enough interpersonal involvement.

The basic insight of the Enneagram is that each of us has a major gift or talent, but that its overuse can turn it into a compulsion by midlife. The five's gift is an intellectual bent whose ultimate fulfillment is wisdom. One problem that surfaces when this gift becomes an unconscious drive is that the five fears never knowing enough, seeking more and more knowledge, which results in an inability to take action. I could relate to the never-knowing-enough feeling. When I prepared the section of whatever literature I had assigned for homework, I often did extensive searches to find the exact meaning of every abstruse term I came across. My fear was that at least one student would question me about the meaning and derivation of the word. It turned out to be mainly an exercise in self-education. As it turned out, I was just grateful if the students actually read the assignment—or at least part of it. I might have spent that research time better by taking a vigorous walk.

I also developed the habit of reading long philosophical, psychological, and spiritual works. I waded through Ernest Becker's tome, *The Denial of Death*. Perhaps it is necessary for "head" types (as fives, sixes, and sevens are categorized) to do this sort of thing. It seemed necessary for Becker to write such a long volume in order to arrive at the peace of a simplified view of life. The quotation that I best remember from his long work is "Childlike foolishness is the true calling of the mature man"—a statement found near the end of his lengthy, scholarly study.

The "unredeemed" five tends to hoard, storing up unshared knowledge. Although teaching allowed me to share some of the insights I had acquired through reading, my students were teenagers/young adults, whereas I had begun to fill my notebooks with thoughts for more mature years. Reading had always been deeply enriching for me. Reflecting upon the insights of the Enneagram, I began to wonder if I had wandered so far into the forest of books that I was losing sight of where I was headed. Perhaps some lines from T. S. Eliot that I had copied down years before in my first notebook best expressed my feelings: "Like a child who has wandered into a forest/playing with an imaginary playmate and suddenly discovers he is only a child/lost in a forest, wanting to go home."

Six

Coming to My Senses

The theories of the Myers-Briggs and the Enneagram were helpful, but all theory needs practical application for personal development. Ernest Becker, in *The Denial of Death*, came to a simple vision comparable to the condition insisted upon by Jesus, "Unless you become like little children, you shall not enter the kingdom of heaven." Perhaps at the end of all theories and conjectures lies a synthesis, a wholeness beyond abstraction and analysis. For some of us—fives, anyway—the process of tracking it all down and sorting through things is a necessary part of the path. My first notebook contains lines from Sr. Maris Stella's poem entitled "Riddles": "Out of this tangle of threads to find the thread that will untangle the threads. Out of this maze to find the amazing path and so be led back to the beginning by incredible ways." The poem describes a process of moving through complexity to simplicity. I found a similar pattern in T. S. Eliot's "The Four Quartets." Here the poet leads us through a maze of reflections to arrive at "a condition of complete simplicity, costing not less than everything."

The gift of fives can be realized by linking abstract knowledge to a search for wisdom and heart knowledge. Instead of hoarding, we need to share what we have learned in the context of engaged, related living. Interaction with friends provided me with a way to make the Enneagram practical. The theory divides the nine types into three categories: head types, gut types and heart types. I was a head type, but had two friends whose types were in the other two categories. When we went out to dinner, or on vacation, we made decisions together. With input from all three categories, we made choices that we rarely regretted.

Reflecting upon the withdrawal factor of fives, I began to wonder why I behaved like an observing owl at meetings, rarely contributing to the discussions. Perhaps I had been discouraged from speaking up by many people who transgressed a dictum from one of my notebooks: "Blessed is he [or she] who, having nothing to say, does not give wordy evidence of the fact." Or I might have taken to heart the dim view of noisy owls described by Edward Lear:

> There was an old person of Crowle
> Who lived in the nest of an owl.
> When they screamed in the nest, he screamed out with the rest,
> That depressing old person of Crowle.

In any case, I decided to attempt to speak up more at meetings. I was uncomfortable at first, but I found that I did have something to contribute. In fact, I found it to be acceptable (to some) to make a humorous remark when discussions became overly serious. I myself was grateful when someone in a group lightened things up a bit—for example, the teacher who spoke up at a particularly grim faculty meeting. The principal of that school had decided to solve the problem of colorful graffiti in one of the boys' restrooms by locking the doors for an indefinite period of time. Not believing in collegiality, he put a large "CLOSED" sign on the door without explanation. The teacher, who sympathized with the boys' frustrating trek to another building, raised his hand at the meeting and asked, "About the boys' restroom in my building—is it a mural?"

Compounding my "fiveness" in Enneagram terms was the fact that I tested out as a "J" on the Myers-Briggs. Although "J" stands for "judgment," it does not mean judgmental, but is used to describe people whose attitude toward taking action in the world shows a preference for planning, orderliness, regulation, control, and closure. The opposite preference is designated "P," standing for "perception." This type prefers to keep options open and to live more flexibly and spontaneously, trying to understand rather than control. A typical example given to show the difference is that a "J" is always early for an appointment or meeting, assuming one should be there ten minutes ahead of time, whereas a "P" thinks of the scheduled time of the meeting as the time to start moving toward it. By midlife the danger is that either type may become too extreme and needs to move toward the other preference for balance. Richard Rohr tells the story of a sister who worked on a project with him. Becoming frustrated with his desire to make quick decisions and move on, she said, "Richard, let me P on your J."

By midlife I found myself planning and replanning for classes, attempting to anticipate any problem that might arise. I was given classes of students who needed to improve elementary skills, and I began to be obsessed with details and objective facts—never my strong suit. Since reading and writing skills were declining steadily, secondary schools tried to shoulder the burden of teaching basics once covered at the grammar school level. The overplanning and the marathon of correcting English papers took precedence over my living in the present moment. I began to feel that I might be "in the know" but was less and less in the now. As soon as one thing was planned and put into action, my mind sailed off to prepare for the next. I felt that I had to cover every detail of historical or factual material. My work was organized, but not much fun.

The situation reminded me of a cartoon I once saw on the back of a short-lived but thought-provoking magazine entitled *The Critic*. The first frame shows a planet with a happy, simple little creature sitting on top of it smelling a flower and admiring a circling butterfly. In the next frame another planet, which is divided into compartments, moves into view. On top of it sits a creature in full armor, scowling at the other planet. As the strip continues, the Martian planet moves closer and closer. In the last frame, the first planet and its simple occupant appear to have shrunk and are imprisoned in one of the compartments of the organized planet. No captions were necessary.

Reflecting upon the cartoon, I wondered if I had become lost in abstraction and out of touch with the world of the senses. I thought back to my childhood, trying to remember sensory experiences. A spring scene in our backyard came to mind. I had just recovered from a cold. It was wonderful to be able to go outside. I walked down to the back of the yard and stood in front of the roses. The sun felt warm on my back. The roses were a delicate pink. I felt much better and sensed myself relaxing into a peaceful state. Another scene returned. I was waiting in the car on the side street next to a grocery store. My mother had gone in. I sat listening to the soft patter of raindrops on the top of the car—I liked it. Another memory was of the "tule fog" in Fresno, ground fog, sometimes so dense that visibility is limited to a few feet. I was outside on my tricycle on a foggy day. I loved the way the fog made things disappear, mysteriously creating around me a little white room, a private space that I could be in, without having to see all of the street or neighborhood. It was a comforting sort of feeling—like being outside and inside at the same time. I knew that if I got too cold I could go inside where it was warm and there were people, but I enjoyed being outside in my own little place, surrounded by the expanse of fog for a while.

In contrast, the summer temperatures in Fresno often soar above 100 degrees. Many people who drive through the area in the summer months seem to think the heat to be a permanent condition, making it a good place to avoid. One infrequent visitor suggested the city should be called "Hell Town." As children, one way we adapted to the season was by developing "tough soles," enabling us to go barefoot on the sizzling sidewalks and asphalt—something I would never try again.

Down the street lived a family with a boy and girl around our ages. The father sold candy and other items, which he bought wholesale and kept in their basement—an unusual feature in a Fresno house. On scorching summer days we escaped the heat by retreating into the intriguing basement to lie down on the cool cement. Once we found a case of Luden's cough drops, each box melted into a single bumpy bar. We had to force the contents out, and then lick it as if it were a sucker without a stick. The medicinal taste reminded me of the savory, pungent odor of the geranium leaves we soaked to make perfume. But usually the cough drop sucker lost its appeal halfway through. Real candy was better.

Another vivid memory returned—that of our primary readers at school. The bookmakers had generously supplied these textbooks with brightly colored division pages between the stories. I remember my delight at seeing a whole page of red—no writing, no pictures, just a solid beautiful rectangle of red. There were also blue ones and green ones. I was fascinated, just staring at the brilliance of the colors. These pages seemed so far superior to the ones with writing on them that I would have gladly just skipped the reading part of the lesson.

Appreciation of the physical world had not always been foreign to me, but by midlife sensory experience had become, in Myers-Briggs terms, my "inferior function," designated by the letter "S." People whose dominant function is sensing focus on the external world of literal, realistic facts and details. They approach tasks in a step-by-step sequential manner. Those of us with sensing as an inferior function, however, sometimes find factual, sequential details to be overwhelming since we have developed imaginative, figurative approaches to life, jumping to conclusions through intuitive hunches. Learning about my inferior function threw some light upon my early difficulties with arithmetic, or detailed factual procedures of any kind. As a teacher, I became aware that I often made mistakes writing page numbers on the board; usually I had the correct numerals, but confused the order. Finally, I began telling my classes that since words were "my thing" I wasn't good at numbers and asked the students to tell me if I slipped up. I also frequently made errors writing and recording check numbers. When I finally had occasion to be the house bookkeeper, I approached each working session with dread and probably labored over it three times longer than it would have taken a dominant sensor. I wasn't dyslexic; my mind just wandered away from the numbers too easily.

Dominate sensate types delight in the outer world. Inferior sensors focus mainly on the inner world, and therefore have tendencies to trip over furniture and generally disregard details in the outer world. By the time I was in college, I had gained some experience as a baby sitter and was hired by a couple I hadn't sat for previously. While they were out, the doorbell rang. I opened the door to a man who wanted to see the husband. I explained that the couple had gone out, and he went away. After the parents returned, I told them about the incident. They asked me detailed questions about the man: was he walking or driving? What did he look like? What was he wearing? I couldn't answer any of their questions, not having taken in any of the details. They didn't call me again. Maybe they suspected that I might not remember what I was doing there or even which room the baby was in. My sister once told me that she thought it wasn't a good idea for me to wander around a large store of any kind while she was shopping. She thought I might drift off into a corner, sit down, and reflect. Then it would be quite a chore for her to find me. I left home at nineteen, still having to ask my mother where things belonged in the kitchen drawers.

The plight of the inferior sensor reminds me of another scene in *The Phantom Tollbooth*. Milo, the young hero, meets a boy called Alec Bings, who "sees through things"—an obvious intuitive. He tells Milo and his companions that he can see "whatever is inside, behind, around, covered by or subsequent to anything else." The drawback, he tells them, is that he isn't able to see whatever is right in front of him. As he leads the others through the Forest of Sight, he himself keeps bumping into the trees.

Alec tells Milo that many people live in a wonderful city there called Reality. When Milo sees a beautiful city beyond the trees of the forest, he says, "Is that it?" Alec explains that what Milo is looking at is the City of Illusions, and that they are now standing in the middle of the main street of Reality, but the city has become invisible. Years ago, he tells them, people had taken pleasure in looking at the city as they walked from place to place, but they discovered that they could avoid distractions and walk faster by looking at their shoes. As a result, the beauty and wonder of the city began to disappear until no one could see any of it, because no one cared. Now many of them live in Illusions.

As a child I had a recurring nightmare about a red carpet in the closet. I found myself standing at the door of the closet. The interior was dark, except for the bright red rug. I knew that the carpet would suck me down into it like quicksand, even before it happened. There was nothing I could do to prevent it from pulling me down. A compulsion drew me toward it; then the carpet itself dragged me down. Before I was pulled all the way in, I always woke up. The red carpet most likely symbolized for me the physical world of the senses, of the body. The carpet was the color of blood; my reactions in the dream were more instinctual than rational. I had developed a degree of fear of the physical world, partly as a result of the dualism in the church teaching of that time. The body was considered to be inferior to the soul, as was the material world to the spiritual, and earthly life to that of heaven. We were taught to curb desires, to rise above things, and to "offer up" physical and mental difficulties. "Mind over matter" was a familiar phrase. Sexual feelings and impure thoughts were considered the worst sins.

Although I had already a natural inclination toward an inner reflective mode of development, hearing the physical world disparaged regularly fed my distrust of it. Of course, whatever is prohibited or rejected holds a certain fascination. We had on our bookshelf a copy of Dante's *Inferno*, vividly illustrated with lithographs by Gustav Dore. When my parents weren't looking, I used to sneak the book off the shelf to marvel at the crowds of writhing, naked bodies that were displayed undergoing the many tortures of hell. In retrospect, I remember there being more men than women in hell, but perhaps my memory reflects my curiosity at that time.

The moral training of the time encouraged us to sublimate our physical, instinctive tendencies. I chose to direct my energies toward self-control and unselfishness after hearing a sermon about not fighting with your sister or brother over a toy. I tried out the idea later that week when my sister and I were playing tug of war with a toy, but let go of it so fast that she fell down. As I was growing up, I became acquainted with the Catholic disciplinary practices of abstaining from meat on Fridays, refraining from food (even water) before Holy Communion, and observing the ascetical practices of Advent and Lent. Whatever candy came our way during Lent we stored in a large jar on the top of the refrigerator. At noon on Holy Saturday, it was open candy season. What with the saved up candy and the new Easter candy, some of us overate, and ironically did more penance by feeling sick on Easter Sunday.

Before I entered religious life, I had read a number of Catholic authors—Fulton Sheen, Thomas à Kempis and others. I frequently took books out of our parish library. Some of them described more refined forms of asceticism, such as custody of the eyes. I practiced this for a while, not letting myself look at things in each room of the house as I passed through. By midlife, however, I was missing a lot of scenery, and needed to reverse directions, to start looking again.

Not being aware of the material world has its pitfalls. A. A. Milne describes an analogous situation in *Winnie the Pooh*. One day Pooh plans to trap a Heffalump. He suggests to Piglet that they build a "Very Deep Pit" to catch it. Piglet is not convinced of the success of the idea and asks, "Why would he fall in?" In answer, "Pooh rubbed his nose with his paw, and said that the Heffalump might be walking along, humming a little song, looking up at the sky, wondering if it would rain, and so he wouldn't see the Very Deep Pit until he was halfway down, when it would be too late." Pooh must have counted on meeting a Heffalump with an inferior sensing function.

Inferior sensors are prone to take two extreme attitudes toward the body as a part of the physical world. One is to ignore some aspects of it, as Heffalumps might. This extreme can result in being unaware of the need for a balance in sensual pleasures. Naomi Quenk describes this problem in her book *Beside Ourselves*. She deals with the hidden personalities that are the result of unconscious, shadow elements. Quenk states that inferior sensors may binge or overeat. "They see themselves as obsessively doing harm to their bodies. A typical tactic is to overindulge compulsively, and immediately after—if not during the episode— berate themselves for their uncontrolled, shallow, destructive behavior." The result is a paralyzing state of impasse. The internalized negative mother's voice says, "You shouldn't have done that." Then the negative father's voice cements the feeling of guilt by saying, "But you did do it— and now it's too late." Winnie the Pooh gets himself in a similar situation when he visits his friend Rabbit and eats up all the honey in the rabbit hole. Pooh grows so fat that he gets stuck in Rabbit's front door hole. Rabbit himself, finding "the front door full" goes out the back and around to tell Pooh, "I didn't like to say anything…one of us was eating too much…and I knew it wasn't *me*." There was nothing for it, but that Pooh stay there a week until he got thinner. By midlife my thought had become weightier, and my body, being somewhat ignored, followed suit. I not only needed to go on a diet, but to incorporate some regular exercise into my life. As Milne's Edward Bear says, "A bear, however hard he tries, grows tubby without exercise."

The other extreme that inferior sensors can fall into is obsessing about the body, fearing physical diseases without actually consulting doctors or obtaining factual information. During a school vacation early in my teaching career when we weren't allowed much travel, I spent most of the time reading and reflecting in the convent where I lived. Having extra time to think and to explore possibilities, I began searching around in my mouth with my tongue. To my horror, I discovered a large lump on the roof of my mouth. I panicked, imagining all sorts of dreadful diseases that I might have. After a few days, I decided not to give up on life and made an appointment with my dentist, who was nearby. He informed me that what I could feel was a bone structure that constituted the top of my mouth. I had been born with it and wouldn't be able to open my mouth without it. I thanked him, then closed my mouth and went home.

An overly emotional reaction is usually a good indication that one's inferior function has been triggered. Marie-Louis Von Franz suggests several questions to ask in identifying a person's inferior function: "What is the greatest cross for the person? Where is his greatest suffering? Where does he feel that he always knocks his head against the obstacle and suffers hell?" When we fall unconsciously into the grip of the inferior function, we feel particularly touchy, sensitive to criticism from others, and overly critical of ourselves. It is the area in which we always fail to be perfect; therefore it can act as a grace by always bringing us to our knees before God. If we had any common sense, we would adopt the humble stance of the publican in the gospel, but most of us attempt to ignore our weaknesses, putting on the righteous air of the Pharisee. In an early notebook I recorded a statement from Gerald Vann that stayed with me: "We must find and face our hell. It should not be too difficult to find."

Being unaware of minor sensory details can also get an inferior sensor into trouble. I remember having misplaced my sunglasses after having driven somewhere in a community car belonging to the provincial house. I knew that I had left them on the dashboard of the car and went back to get them. They were gone. Then I returned to my room, where I had gone directly from the car, and searched up and down. I noticed myself getting out of control, pulling out drawers wildly, looking through all my pockets. I was in a "hissy fit," as one of my friends says. Finally I returned to the parking lot. A whole fleet of cars had been leased for the use of the large community house and almost all of them were the same make and model, but were of different colors. I had forgotten the color of the car I had driven! When I subsequently found the right car, there were my sunglasses where I had left them. A wild scene for nothing? But the experience made me a bit more aware. I wasn't "all there" when it came to details.

Paradoxically, God touches us more through our weaknesses than our strengths. Von Franz states, "The inferior function is the ever bleeding wound of the conscious personality, but through it the unconscious can always come in and so enlarge consciousness and bring forth a new attitude." For example, she indicates that our concern about underdeveloped countries may be a case of projection, triggered by underdeveloped countries within ourselves that need attention, but of which we are unconscious. She compares the four functions to doors in the room of our psyches. "The fourth door of your room is where angels can come in, but also devils."

Her mention of angels that might enter through the inferior function reminded me of Jung's idea about the shadow part of ourselves being almost pure gold. He thought that the neglected energy present in the underdeveloped parts of ourselves can be transformed into vital energy if we are willing to do the necessary work. Jung saw this transformation as having been the true quest of the alchemists, who mistook a pattern proper to psychological transformation for a chemical process that could turn base metal into gold. They were not entirely wrong, but had interpreted a symbolic truth in a literal way.

The undeveloped energy of the inferior function builds up over such a period of years that the "intensity of life is very often much greater there," as Von Franz says. Not only is there the threat of a loss of control in this area, but also an attractive excitement contained there. For an inferior sensor, the physical, sensuous world holds a numinous, magical allure. One cannot fully develop this function, but needs to acknowledge, befriend, and play with its untapped energy.

My reading suggested that one activity that would allow me to dabble and delight in sensing was cooking. My father was a newspaperman in the editorial department and balanced intellectual work with his hobby of gourmet cooking. I relished his delicious entrees and side dishes, but never did much cooking myself. I found that when I took my turn cooking dinner in small convents I seemed to enjoy it. But grocery shopping entailed too many particulars—prices, brands, preferences etc. Just finding things in the store was problematic. As time went on, I began to share my father's enthusiasm for a visit to the grocery store, but not to the extent that he did. He would have liked to have gone every day.

After he retired, he almost did, taking hours to look at everything, pricing items, then driving across town for something three to five cents cheaper. Cantaloupes were his favorite fruit. An expert on choosing them in season, he used to advise others who were shopping about which melons were ripe. They were not to be had in the winter, so he stocked up on them in the summer. Our family dubbed him "the mellonaire." We usually took a four-hour trip to Santa Cruz during his vacation in the summer to visit relatives and enjoy the ocean for a week. One particularly hot summer my father found a good price for ripe melons there and brought a box of them home in the car from the coast. We had no air conditioning, and on the way home the melons exuded an extremely strong odor, which belongs in the category of smells that mother designated as WHIFFY.

One source I read encouraged inferior sensors to engage in cooking for large groups of people, so I signed up several summers to cook for large convents in the north, which also provided me with some travel and a change of scene. My father used to undertake intricate and exotic cooking processes that required early morning chopping and sautéing for sauces and marinades. One summer I tried a few of his recipes, but found it took me all day to prepare the dinner. People enjoyed eating it, but I thought there must be a better way, and developed more simplified recipes of my own. In addition to cooking, I did the shopping. Having come to appreciate the sensory world more, I particularly enjoyed the produce section with its exciting displays of color: yellow, orange, green, red, purple.

Another helpful activity for introverted intuitives is to spend extended periods of time outdoors in beautiful, natural surroundings. When I visited Fresno during Easter vacations, my mother and sister and I began taking trips up into the surrounding foothills to search for wildflowers. The San Joaquin Valley and its hills were once covered with carpets of California poppies in the spring, but since so much of the valley floor has been developed for agriculture and housing, we had to drive up into the foothills to find them. Purple lupine still paints the hills in some places. Swaths of yellow or pink appear where thousands of tiny flowers grow. Fiddleneck lines the lower valley roads. A number of stops are required to get out of the car in order to see the tiny flowers clearly. Usually we had to gaze at them through barbed wire fences that bordered the property owned by farmers whose cows grazed over much of the area.

We always took lawn chairs and a picnic, seeking a spot that wasn't fenced in—preferably a place with a little stream or a trickle of water from the melting snow in the upper elevations. Sometimes my sister brought paints to capture a scene; usually my mother and I brought books. But the best part was just sitting among the wildflowers—like Ferdinand the bull. If cows or bulls were on the scene, they avoided our company. I attempted to describe the experience in a poem:

> If you go far enough
> Through spring foothills
> Toward the mountains
> In April
> Suddenly—wildflowers!
>
> White popcorn flowers scattered on low hills
> Fiddleneck and goldenrod catching the sun,
> Shepherd's purse—slender stems offering small green hearts
>   (with a peppery flavor)
> And miner's lettuce—white candles in green elven cups.

Indian paint brush, yellow violets,
The red bud trees—showers of deep rose on early green,
Washes of daisies, fire poppies,
Then, purple flecked with white, the lupine boldly streaks hills
and meadows.

A sprinkling of smaller things: little low cities of yellow stars
humming with tiny bees.

But the rarest and most beautiful?
Secondly the buttercup (freshest yellow)
Firstly the shy, hiding baby blue-eye
Only a few patches in any year—
Sky blue babies, white-centered, dance on short stems in
sequestered places.

And what of the orange that once covered hills and valleys?
A few poppies remain, reminders of a younger countryside.

Brown cows sit in the middle of it all,
Chewing thoughtfully, listening to the woodpecker's call.

Whatever their personality types, most people need to develop a program of exercise at midlife. My choice was walking. I searched out places of natural beauty, and walked for an hour in the morning when possible. One of my favorite walks is next to a natural lagoon in Los Angeles. Some call it the Grand Canal of the Venice Beach area, but its official name is the Ballona Lagoon. Large houses line either side of the lagoon, but on one side a walking path has been preserved with a fence to allow the vegetation to flourish on the waterside. It is a place with enough stillness to quiet me and more expanse than I can take in at a glance, lest it become humdrum.

The lagoon looks like an empty backwater at low tide, but is teaming with unseen life. Part of the shore is covered with tiny dark conical shells, apparently immobile and uninhabited. On closer observation one day, I noticed a tiny, moist glistening at the larger end of one and realized that it was alive. A steady gaze at the lifeless, murky, water reveals the dark shapes of minnows sweeping the shallows, catching occasional sunbeams like tiny winks of light. A few of the tiny silver fish leap out, then return with a "blip."

The water level depends on the tides. As water rushes in from the ocean culvert, widening waves swell the lagoon, ride in for a while, then merge with the long mirror of water. At high tide, the entire surface smooths. An occasional tern dives in, creating concentric circles which slowly fade, returning a reflection of the sky. Bubbles from the stirring of underwater life appear—then the mirror clears again.

When the tide ebbs, the lagoon narrows. It is feeding time for birds that wade in the water or wait on the shore. The fish moment is all. With surpassing patience, some birds stand still; sandpipers, killdeer and green herons tiptoe along the shore. The egrets are the most elegant, slim white figures contrasting with the dark muddy bank. The great egrets with yellow bills and long black legs stand like statues in the shallows. Smaller egrets with sharp black bills probe the vegetation for tiny creatures which their skinny yellow feet stir up on the water's edge.

In addition to at least four mallards that live there year round, unusual migrating ducks visit, including the charming black and white bufflehead, the smallest American duck. Always there are a few needle-billed, brown speckled snipes poking about. But the most fascinating to me is the belted kingfisher. The female outdoes the male in beauty. She has his angular head, gray feathers with a belt of white, but sports an additional belt of deep chestnut and black. I heard her rattling call for over a year before I spotted her sitting high above the path on a telephone wire where I found her often thereafter. Once in a while larger birds appear. A stately gray-blue heron steps regally along the shore or stands unmoving, alert, staring down from a neck that seems too long for its body. Pelicans sometimes glide above, land in the lagoon to thrash about for fish, and then swallow them dramatically, revealing their yawning, expandable throats.

Along the first part of the trail are high garden walls covered with pink, orange, and magenta bougainvillea. A few abound with jasmine of different kinds. Fragrant honeysuckle fills several borders. Other gardens offer Iceland poppies, Mexican evening primrose, roses, pansies and day lilies. The lagoon side of the path has its own display. When I first discovered the walk, yellow sourgrass, ice plant, and daisies covered most of it. Bindweed, like white morning glories striped with pink, grew along a certain fence near yellow beach primroses. A few California poppies appeared, and Jimsonweed in season—a white, trumpet-shaped flower whose petals narrow to delicate slender tips. It looks good enough to eat, but is actually poisonous. Its beauty is of the kind Georgia O'Keefee has paid tribute to in her impressive paintings of single flowers.

After I started walking the lagoon path, signs went up at intervals on the trail about a petition to restore the area to indigenous vegetation. That spring yellow sourgrass covered most of the shore and daisies grew shoulder high. I hurried down expectantly on a particularly beautiful morning. To my horror, all the plants near the head of the path had been removed! The restoration had begun. A few weeks earlier, I had noticed some machines removing unwanted rocks and a cement remnant of a structure long gone, but hadn't realized that practically the whole shore would be stripped. Some of the flowers I had waited for a year to see again had just started blooming. Now the area was barren, covered with heaps of dredged up mud, silt and broken shells. The small area of bindweed and primroses had been spared but the plentiful, cheerful daisies had been condemned as illegal citizens. Oh no—a whole season without them?

Then the restorers started putting up little colored flags, indicating that seeds had been planted. I applauded their efforts, but still missed the daisies. It just wouldn't be the same. As time went on, I reluctantly became resigned to the situation. The culvert area where the ocean water enters the lagoon was dredged, and an observation deck of new blond wood was built out over it, allowing visitors to see schools of fish moving over the beds of muscles and other encrustations. I walked out on it one day and saw two fascinating sea slugs, each covered with protrusions of delicate, airy veils that quivered in the undercurrent.

For some time I concentrated on other aspects of the walk, trying not to notice the dearth of vegetation on the waterside. In the small patch that had been left untouched, bumble bees and tiny bright green flies circled the bindweed. Noticing a little movement on the mud bank nearby, I stepped closer, but the bank looked empty. Stopping again on the way back, I began to see tiny shapes in constant motion, and watched for a while from a distance. Very small creatures were definitely down there, and seemed to change color from time to time. I went back to the car to get a pair of binoculars and returned. Through the lenses I saw tiny crabs that seemed to be either dancing or fencing with one another in pairs. They advanced, then retreated; one slipped into an unseen hole in the mud, reappeared, and the pattern continued. They were just a shade darker than the brown mud, but every few seconds I could see a bit of white. Holding the glasses steady, I concentrated on one of the tiny crabs. After a couple of seconds, one of its claws began to grow larger, as if it were inflating. In the process, the brown claw became white, as a balloon lightens in color when it expands. I was amazed.

A few days later I visited the local library. Not having an extensive background in science, I tried the children's section where I found a picture book with crabs in it and found out that the ones at the lagoon were fiddler crabs. Although I am a "fiddler" myself and had heard the term "fiddler crab," I had never before seen these interesting creatures. The claws of the males enlarge when they are courting or fighting. I couldn't tell which activity was being enacted on the mud bank, but they had all been enthusiastically engaged in one or the other that morning.

Occasionally at the lagoon I caught glimpses of a Phoebe flycatcher. This winsome little bird has a trim, angular head of black that matches its back and tail feathers. A white underside provides a striking contrast. It perches on a pole or rock, watching intently, then darts out in a circle and back—an unseen fly is gone. Flies seem rather foul food for such a charming creature. Perhaps the Phoebe is a tiny sin eater, I thought, ridding the world of pesky flies, then turning them into charming birds—an alchemical miracle!

During the time that I had turned my attention to crabs and birds, green sprouts began to appear on the bank of the lagoon. Signs were posted at intervals to protect the seedlings: "Keep Out: Entry prohibited due to sensitive habitat and revegetation efforts." Slowly the barren bank was transformed. In the spring, more yellow beach primroses appeared than I could have imagined. Generous patches of owl clover crowded the shore—soft thumbs of fresh magenta, sprinkled with a few white "eyes." Then came poppies, bush lupine, indigenous black-centered yellow daisies, and abundant bindweed. Mysterious plants began to sprout next to little signs that identified them as sandbur, borego bedstraw, coastal prickly pear, sea cliff buckwheat, and coyote melon.

As a result of the dredging, the seawater flowed in smoothly now and filled the entire lagoon at high tide. A watering system along the shoreline was supplied to nurture the growing plants. The weather encouraged the project. It was an El Niño year, which provided more rain than Southern California ever expects. The lagoon was transformed. A metal sculpture celebrating the renewal was put up on the observation deck bearing the words "A Dream Fulfilled: June 6, 1998." When I saw it for the first time, an impressive pelican sailed over, as if in tribute to the success of the restoration.

Seven

Theories and Beyond

In coming to appreciate the beauty and detail of the physical world, I had "gone out of my mind and come to my senses." Having become a little less like Alec Bings, I enjoyed looking at trees instead of bumping into them while lost in thought. Nature provided me with new dimensions to explore. I tracked down gardens, state parks, and beaches whenever I could. Carrying lawn chairs in the car, I could sit for extended periods if the selected spot wasn't good for long walks. During the school year, I took English papers and on vacation, books to read, particularly in the areas of Jungian psychology and spirituality. Much of the reading dealt with the importance of striving for greater consciousness.

The theories suggested that as newly born infants we are relatively unconscious, feeling ourselves to be one with the world around us. This oceanic experience of fusion with our mother and the environment gradually gives way to the development of a separate self or ego, which eventually enables us to function as a particular personality and to take our place in the world. After having established ourselves in a particular vocation, career and lifestyle, we are then called to a more interior journey at midlife in order to discover the unexplored, unconscious parts of ourselves. Having the opportunity to grow beyond mere ego control, and to deepen our relationship with God and others, we may thereby reach a state of oneness with the world that is born of conscious experience.

Contact with our true selves allows us to enjoy a deeper connection with all, without losing our individuality.

A professor I had once likened these three stages of development to a scene at the beach. Some small children play near the water, representing the first stage of oneness with the world. Adults with machines smooth the sand on the beach, exemplifying the role of the developed ego assuming an active role in the world. An old couple sits in a car nearby, consciously observing and appreciating the whole view in a contemplative manner.

Looking back, I began to consider how these concepts had played themselves out in my own life. Pondering the mysterious presence of my grandmother's furniture illuminated in sunlight seemed comparable to the first stage of wonder and oneness. Two earlier memories were related to me by my mother. She was setting the table for a meal; I was in a high chair. She put down a fork, which made a metallic noise as it hit a knife, and I sang out, "Nang!" in imitation. She was astonished, not having realized that I considered myself part of the action. Another time, holding me up in a towel after a bath, she reports that I looked steadily into her eyes and cried, "Mona." She then realized that I must have seen my reflection in her eyes. (I had been educated to recognize my image by being held up to a number of mirrors.) These two tales seem to bear out the concept of an initial state of connectedness.

One example of the next stage of development—that of the separate self—was the traumatic appendectomy I experienced at age five, which necessitated a hospital stay away from home. A tonsillectomy followed a few years later, also requiring overnights in the hospital. Both were painful experiences of separation, but I was seven at the time of the second surgery and able to envision an escape plan. By that time I knew the neighborhood well enough to know the way home. Our house was several blocks away from the hospital. When I was left alone at night, I imagined climbing out of the bed, sneaking down the hall to the front door, and walking home in the hospital gown. I settled for climbing out for a drink of water when the nurses weren't looking. At least that was my plan as I drifted into sleep.

The separation from the original feeling of oneness with the world, although necessary, is a painful process. In addition to the feeling of physical separation, individual differences in maturity and personality separate us. Early experiences of having viewpoints and feelings that differ from one's parents can result in guilt feelings, as I had found out in my struggles with "niceness training." I eventually learned to be polite, but perhaps on the whole I overdid it, as did many women of my time. The balance between developing good manners and maintaining an ability to express one's feelings is a difficult challenge.

When my niece Francesca was a baby, her vociferous reaction to being denied her older brother's ice cream cone attracted the attention of a well-meaning but unrealistic woman nearby who said to her, "Nice girls don't scream." I knew from experience that sometimes nice girls screamed interiorly, if not allowed to express themselves to some degree. As David Richo writes, "Part of being polite is not to show our feelings because it may make others uncomfortable. Politeness is often the opposite of feeling." Perhaps the pendulum has swung too far in the opposite direction from polite behavior. "Letting it all hang out" is the motto of innumerable TV talk shows, and problems in the discipline of the young have escalated. In any case, the struggle to develop a separate self is an arduous task for both child and parents.

Adolescents experience a poignant loneliness particular to their age when the necessary separation from their parents intensifies. Although teenagers attempt to merge with others in peer groups to alleviate their dilemma, they spend much time in daydreaming and reflecting on future possibilities. As one poet wrote, "The thoughts of the young are long, long thoughts." At the end of my eighth grade year, although our class celebrated our graduation together, I found myself walking home alone on the last day. At the public junior high that I attended, sophisticated practices more appropriate for the college level had developed—such as belonging to sororities. I felt the groups were artificial and cliquey and just wasn't interested. My friends were all in groups that had parties that day. Walking home alone felt strange at the time, but it gave me the feeling that one had to pay a price to be an individual.

At the end of high school I had developed enough musical skills on the violin to win a scholarship to Fresno State College as a music major. Two years later, I entered the convent, eventually completing the major. Ironically, at the time in life when most people develop an ego that can take its place in the outer world, I responded to a vocation that required submission and a degree of anonymity. I wasn't interested in becoming an elementary school teacher, but following orders was a given in religious life. My independent thinking became somewhat a submarine life, in which I secretly planted radish seeds and read non-best sellers. I surfaced occasionally, sometimes having a brush with authorities who hadn't been reading the same material.

The changes in religious life following Vatican II encouraged more positive ego development in religious women. The paradigms for spiritual development, formulated by men who had been influenced by the culture of the Western world, were no longer adequate. Ancient myths in which the hero sacrificed a bull or killed the Minotaur symbolized the taming of an aggressive masculine ego bent on power. But women had been brought up to be nonassertive and docile in our culture. Rather than becoming more submissive, women needed to develop the assertiveness required to establish a healthy ego before the time came for relinquishing it to the greater Self (Spirit) in the third stage of development. Some brands of feminism merely imitated the male pattern. For modern women's development, it seemed that a new spirituality was called for. Passivity was passé and detrimental.

When I was in my mid-fifties, I began teaching at the college level. In order to do so I had to complete a master's degree that I had once begun. The dilemma of the feminine in our time was uppermost in my mind, so I chose for my thesis a study of the feminine perspective as a mode of teaching literature. It was a way to clarify the problem for myself, using the insights I had gained in both literature and psychology.

By that time I had discovered that our culture has greatly overemphasized masculine qualities. Although positive masculine traits include strength, assertiveness, action, discernment and differentiation, this excessive focus has called forth the negative masculine. As Gareth Hill points out, "Order and organization for their own sake lead to complacency, rigidity, dehumanizing righteousness, inauthenticity, pettiness, brittleness, dryness and lifelessness." He suggests that the authoritarian administration and the rigid parents in the 1989 film "Dead Poets Society" embody negative masculine traits, whereas the sensitive, caring male teacher and the artistic, responsive male student exhibit positive feminine qualities.

Gilda Lerner's view is that masculine concepts are so imbedded in our culture that they have become invisible through familiarity. This imbalance has resulted in the devaluation of feminine values, such as receptivity, responsiveness, nurturance, wholeness and contemplation. Helen Luke has stated that it is time "to turn from this hidden contempt for feminine values and to cease to identify creativity solely with the products of thought and achievements in the outer world." She insists that one "who quickly responds with intense interest and love to people, to ideas, and to things, is as deeply and truly creative as one who always seeks to lead, to act, to achieve." In fact, she maintains that the "feminine qualities of receptivity, of nurturing in silence and secrecy are…as essential to creation as their masculine opposites and in no way inferior."

All the sources I tapped indicated that the general denigration of feminine attributes has impoverished men as well as women. Apparently, even a successful campaign for achieving women's rights and equality will not restore the balance since the cultural problem for all in the West is the loss of feminine values. The insights of these authors led me to believe that a purely masculine approach to literature does not plumb the depths of great works. We have become readers seeking only facts, information, plot lines, and objective descriptions. Poetry, metaphor and myth require a receptive and responsive reader who engages the work in a relational manner, a stance from the realm of the feminine.

The women of the Western world in the first half of the twentieth century have faced a double bind. On the one hand, we were taught to imitate unbalanced negative masculine qualities—order for order's sake, rigidity, etc. On the other, it seemed that we were expected to embrace the seemingly feminine, but actually undeveloped, qualities of a dependent personality. The proper role of a woman was to be that of a passive, patriarchal, daughter/child. The dependent personality is one that has difficulty initiating projects and working independently. This type volunteers service to gain others' approval and tends to identify strongly with whatever group to which he/she belongs—family, church etc.

Sandra Schneiders, among others, deals with the problems resulting from women's having followed a masculine path of spiritual development. She writes, "Men have taught women to beware of specifically male vices: pride, aggression, disobedience to lawful authority, homosexuality, lust, and the like. Women have rarely been alerted to those vices to which their socialization prompts them, for example: weak submissiveness, fear, self-hatred, jealousy, timidity, self-absorption, small-mindedness, submission of personal identity, and manipulation." The vices she refers to are among those that could be considered negative feminine qualities. Whereas positive masculine traits had taken a negative form as a result of overemphasis, the potentially positive feminine qualities had also taken a negative form, but as a result of neglect and lack of development. What was needed was not just a new spirituality for women, but a restoration of balance through a spirituality that values the positive feminine dimensions in both men and women.

Drawn to a study of Jungian psychology because of its spiritual dimension, I found that Jungian concepts illumined traditional spirituality in a fresh, original way. A convergence of spirituality and Jungian insights began appearing in books by major spiritual writers. Then, amazingly enough, the heretofore totally objective, factual, materialistic world that the sciences had created gave way to a growing awareness of a spiritual dynamic in the cosmos.

Books like *The Tao of Physics* and *Dancing Wu Li Masters* had been on the shelves for some time, along with *The Tao of Pooh* and *The Te of Piglet*. I started with the Pooh and Piglet approaches and ended up reading a number of works by Ken Wilber concerning transpersonal psychology. Finding references to Wilber in a variety of books, I acquired *Up from Eden* and then *A Brief History of Everything* (a formidable title). Wilber certainly doesn't leave much of the universe out of his considerations. I kept these two books on my shelf for over a year before attempting to read them. Although I had ordered paperback editions, both were heavy volumes, containing weighty material.

Up From Eden is subtitled "A Transpersonal View of Human Evolution." Peeking tentatively at the index, I found a number of references to one of my earliest conundrums—original sin. Curiosity prodded the Catholic cat in me to look inside. His breadth of knowledge in multiple disciplines posed quite a challenge. The experience was similar to my struggle to read *Treasure Island* when I was ten. I kept going, even though I found it required much stopping to figure out what I had just read. In approaching the Wilber books, I was tempted to resort to the attitude expressed by a phrase we used in high school: "Let's not. And say we did." However, I persevered, and rather than being completely overwhelmed, was greatly enriched by new insights to ponder.

Wilber sees the Fall, to which we attribute original sin, as an evolutionary "fall upwards" into consciousness. He begins by tracking evolution through the ages, suggesting that the process of evolution entails the movement from "translation to transformation." Using the analogy of a many-storied building, he suggests that moving furniture around or remodeling parts of one floor would be "translation," whereas building another floor above that one would exemplify "transformation."

Nature evolves in the latter manner biologically. When one "floor" becomes inadequate, there is a shift up to another level, which raises the whole structure, while retaining the lower floors as a support for the new floor. Humans develop psychologically and spiritually in the same manner, as transformations move us to higher levels of consciousness.

With this premise in mind, Wilber charts our history in terms of the evolutionary process of moving upward. To greatly oversimplify, he traces cultural development from the primitive instinctual state of prehistoric existence, through the stage of the nomadic magical participation of hunting societies, to a "mythic membership" state of agrarian peoples who eventually founded cities ruled by kings. Then follows the rise of individual consciousness, a stage that he refers to as "mental-egoic," symbolized by myths of the hero who slays the dragon. The hero symbolizes the ego; the dragon, the uroboros, or unconscious matriarchal world of the Great Mother. The emergence of the hero/ego heralded the coming of the Patriarchy—a shift from the world of instinctual bodily existence to the world of the Father, which focuses on discipline and control by means of the intellect and will. In other words, cultural development moved upward from primeval instinct toward the "higher" world of the spirit.

Like Wilber, a number of other authors see the Garden of Eden myth to be symbolic of humankind's growth in consciousness. For example, in *The Eden Project* James Hollis writes "In moving from the Tree of Life, or life instinctively connected, to the Tree of Knowledge, which is the birth of civilization, the race moves from the intimate familiarity of like with like to a strickened consciousness" caused by apparent separation. He suggests that the truth expressed in the myth might also reflect the separation from our mothers that we experience in physical birth— a trauma from which we perhaps never fully recover. Significantly, the account found in the Genesis myth has counterparts in all mythologies.

In a retreat talk I had heard a vignette about a little boy who, after his new baby sister was brought home, ran into the room and said to her,

"Quick—tell me where we come from—I'm beginning to forget." Any story beginning "once upon a time…" conjures up the feeling of a special place somewhere outside of time or before time began. Even the phrase I remember from a rather silly children's recording has a wistful feeling, "Once upon a time, in the Land of the Lemon Drops, six times around the whole world…."

However, Wilber identifies a major problem in the way Western culture has evolved in an upward direction. In terms of his analogy of a many-storied building, a desirable process of evolution includes and integrates the lower floors. The pathology of unbalance that we experience today is the result of having repressed, devalued, and oppressed the lower levels in transcending them. Rather than differentiating bodily, instinctive physical life from that of the mind-spirit, we have disassociated the two, causing the split know as dualism. The tragic effects of this splitting up of reality have prompted the universal search for wholeness.

Everything I had been reading seemed to be indicating that sin and evil in the world were somehow the result of divisiveness, splitting, disassociation and separation. The Whole or Good, on the other hand, seemed related to a state of connectedness or conscious unity. Modern scientific insights regarding the connectedness of the universe offered healing from an unexpected direction. The concept of the "holon" seems to be an antidote to our overemphasis on the idea of hierarchy in nature and society. According to Diarmuid O'Murchu in *Quantum Theology*, a holon is the term for "each whole thing within nature…a whole made of its own parts, yet itself part of a larger whole…each holon must assert its individuality…but also submit to the demands of the whole…a human being, a nation, an ecosystem are all holons." Problems arise when, as Wilber writes, "an arrogant holon doesn't want to be both a whole and a part; it wants to be a whole, period…not…a mutual part of something larger than itself." It wants to dominate other holons, rather than to relate to them.

Although the idea of original sin has been discounted by some as an old-fashioned notion, I found a number of serious authors to be addressing the topic. For example, Willigis Jäger, in *Search for the Meaning of Life*, sums up valuable insights about original sin from the viewpoint of current spirituality:

> All religions know about the imperfect condition of humanity. Many speak of a "fall," of "original sin" but original sin is not a fall from a higher state of consciousness into a more imperfect state. Rather, it is the emergence from a "pre-personal heaven," an awakening from the dullness of the pre-conscious into an ego-experience, a shift out of the state of instinct into the knowledge of good and evil, as the Scripture says. This was a great step forward in evolution, but it also brought with it the whole burden that is bound up with the ego-experience, namely, the experience of sickness, suffering, guilt, loneliness, and death.

The implication of his train of thought is that the effects of original sin are not punishments for a particular action, but are part of the nature of human life. The feeling of separation from the Whole or from God makes human limitations seem to be punishments, because deep down we are intuitively aware that we are connected to the Divine. If our image of God is anthropomorphic, we see God as a Big Person, a Parent, and feel that we must have brought these punishments upon ourselves by having displeased the Parent God.

The Good News is that we were never separated from God, nor ever could be, since God is the ground of our existence. This good news is what Jesus revealed—that the kingdom is within us, and that each of us is a child of God. When he said, "He who sees me, sees the Father," the implication is that God can be seen in any of his children.

Long ago it had seemed to me that original sin got people in trouble. Now it seemed that the people who take God's good news seriously get into trouble, as did Jesus. St. John of the Cross, a master of the interior life, was thrown in jail for taking Jesus seriously. His contemporary, St. Teresa of Avila, was given a certificate of bad conduct by the papal nuncio. Even the profound writings of Meister Eckhart, dealing with the reality of the indwelling God, were condemned and suppressed for many years after his death.

It is the illusion of being an unprotected, separate self threatened by suffering and death that causes the panic in us which Hollis describes as a "stricken consciousness." Jesus' statement about he who would save his life will lose it and vice versa applies here. Beatrice Bruteau states that all sins are forms of trying to preserve our own lives because we believe that if we don't, they won't be preserved. She sees this idea as coming from the Father of Lies and as being the falsehood underlying all sin. She writes, "It is sometimes said that the root of sin is wanting to be God in your own right. There is nothing wrong with wanting to be divine." God desires to share divine life with us. It is our desire to have divine life in our own right that is wrong. This attitude betrays our belief that our only safety lies in controlling everything ourselves. It may appear to be pride, but Bruteau sees this attitude as really fear, "terrible, rock-bottom, existential fear."

Ken Wilber calls our drive toward ego control the Atman Project. He uses the Hindu term "Atman" as referring to "ever-present and ultimate wholeness in men and women." Wilber argues that all we really desire is wholeness, but we fear not only physical death, but also the death to our separate egos that wholeness demands. We have an intuition that our "deepest nature is *already* God," but insist that our egos *should* be God. Therefore, we grasp at a pseudo wholeness through manipulation, attempting to create our own divinity, security and immortality.

Historically, these efforts have taken such forms as storing up food supplies, creating and hoarding money, and building monumental tombs. The human sacrifices of the matriarchal era Wilber sees as efforts to appease the Earth Mother. The hope was that she would be satisfied with the given blood offerings, and let humans off the mortal hook by supplying good harvests that would extend the lives of the worshippers. The heroic age followed, giving rise to the worship of Apollo, the god of reason and logic. This transfer of devotion delivered us from the irrational world of the Mother (mater/matter), and constituted the beginning of the patriarchal era. It was originally a step upward in collective human development, but unfortunately became, as Wilber writes, "a new twist in the Atman project that saw immortality in abstract thought and...unfettered ego expansion." The body then became a threat to the project. The feminine was seen as a threat to the masculine. Thus a dualism was created that was passed down the generations to our own. Men were seen as superior to women, the mind more exalted than the body, the spiritual higher than the physical, and action preferable to being, etc.

A retreat director in the novitiate once told us, "Humility is the ability to make the subtle distinction between ourselves and God." Mistaking the ego for God is a perennial problem. Jäger writes, "The ego is only a little disk swimming on the surface of our total consciousness. It is only one organ of total consciousness. But it acts as if it were the actual commander, and so it's in constant conflict with the depths of our being." The authors of *From Image to Likeness* reiterate, "Sin...would seduce us into the blasphemous thought that 'if God is, I am not; if I am, God is not.'"

I often used verses from *Archy and Mehitabel* in my English classes. The book is a compilation of the work of Don Marquis, who wrote for the New York *Sun*. The verses are supposed to have been written by a cockroach called Archy who typed them at night when the newspaper office was deserted. He jumped head downward on the keys, but lacking the dexterity to press the shift key, he never used punctuation or capital letters. Part of his verse on "warty bliggens the toad" reflects the experience of the inflated ego exaggerating its place in the universe:

> do not tell me
> said warty bliggens
> that there is not a purpose
> in the universe
> the thought is blasphemy
> a little more
> conversation revealed
> that warty bliggens
> considers himself to be
> the center of the said
> universe
> the earth exists
> to grow toadstools for him
> to sit under
> the sun to give him light
> by day and the moon
> and wheeling constellations
> to make beautiful
> the night for the sake of
> warty bliggens

Archy then asks the toad why he is so specially treated by the Creator. Has he done something wonderful to merit such attention? To which Warty replies:

> ask rather...
> what the universe
> has done to deserve me

Archy concludes that humans shouldn't laugh too much at Warty:

> for similar
> absurdities
> have only too often
> lodged in the crinkles
> of the human cerebrum

The consciousness promoted by the patriarchy enabled us to rise above a primitive, unconscious bond with nature, but eventually began to move us further and further away from the physical world into abstraction. The conscious ego, thinking itself to be God, began creating a controllable, abstract universe. The physical universe was looked upon as being measurable, subject to categorization and domination—but as potentially dangerous, if left to its own devices.

The distrust of the corporeal world was reflected in the moral teaching of many religions. Exhortations to avoid sin of a physical, measurable, or sexual nature took precedence, obscuring more subtle forms of selfishness and self-deception in the realm of the mind and attitudes. Hence the possible incomprehensibility of Jesus' suggestion that to look at a woman with adulterous intentions was tantamount to physical adultery. Equally baffling might be his statement about the great difficulty of a rich man's entering the kingdom of heaven, if "riches" refer to attitudes of attachment toward wealth or talent that could separate one from God.

The physical universe became the enemy, to be controlled by the mind and will. The world of the Pharisee was created, in which following the rules was believed to be the way to achieve perfection—a do-it-yourself holiness, which set one apart as righteous and superior to others, rather than as related to them, or to God. In the parable about the Pharisee in the temple, the tax collector realizes his dependence on God. The Pharisee doesn't need God—he's done everything right on his own.

And he certainly wouldn't want to be seen with the tax collector, much less to relate to him.

Great literature yields similar insights. In *The Inferno*, Dante travels down through the circles of hell to find Satan in the bottom pit, which is a region of ice. Helen Luke describes the image as expressing "A cold and cruel egotism, gradually striking inward till even the lingering passions of hatred and destruction are frozen into immobility—this is the final state of sin." In relationship to paradise, Satan is positioned head downwards, symbolizing the ultimate perversion of the intellect, whose proper function is the perception of truth. Dante shows Satan as having three faces, symbolizing the divisions within himself. In each mouth he eternally chews upon a traitor—Judas, Brutus, and Cassius. All three of these men had betrayed friends.

Luke suggests that evil is nourished by "the betrayal of conscious personal love between single individuals." She writes, "The final treachery to God and the Universe is the setting up of a principle [abstract truth] as of more moment than mature love." Two twentieth century poets agree. In his play, *Murder in the Cathedral*, T. S. Eliot writes, "This is the greatest treason—to do the right thing for the wrong reason." William Blake states, "A truth that's told with bad intent/beats all the lies you can invent."

These readings indicate that Satan, Evil personified, is called the Father of Lies because he is the master of illusion and mind games. I found the same portrayal of evil in J. R. R. Tolkien's fantasy trilogy, *Lord of the Rings*. The Enemy of good in Middle-Earth is Sauron, the Dark Lord, who plans to take over the world through his evil Ring of Power. The small hobbit-hero, Frodo, takes on the task of destroying the Ring by returning it to the place where it was originally forged, in the Cracks of Doom, part of Sauron's stronghold. When the Ring is destroyed, the illusory world of the Dark Lord collapses and dissolves, emptying the battlefield of all the evil creatures under Sauron's control, and enabling the true king to return.

The fearsome army the Dark Lord commands becomes disoriented when separated from his control, from the mind that had created the web of illusion. Of the destruction of the Ring, Tolkien writes "The Power that drove them on and filled them with hate and fury was wavering, its will was removed from them...the power of Mordor was scattering like dust in the wind. As when death smites the swollen brooding thing that inhabits their crawling hill and holds them all in sway, ants will wander witless and purposeless and then feebly die, so the creatures of Sauron, orc or troll or beast spell-enslaved, ran thither and thither mindless."

Archibald McLeish's verse play *The Fall of the City* also shows how a self-destructive illusion can be created by irrational fears that play tricks on the mind. A messenger brings news that an enemy is approaching the city, intending to kill or enslave its citizens. Throughout the play, people pass the word along, cowering, wondering what will happen. As the news spreads, it exaggerates until the people feel incapable of defending themselves. Finally, they despair and decide to surrender. When the enemy enters the city, the citizens discover that their enemy is only a single individual—not even human, but merely an empty suit of armor. The people had been defeated by their own fearful imaginations, which separated them from both their inner and outer resources. One phantom enemy easily conquered a city of helpless individuals who might have held off an army had they united in a common endeavor.

In the field of science the overemphasis on the mind and its powers had also been divisive. Theoretical concepts came to be valued to such an extent that they began to take on a life of their own, separated from the realities that they attempted to describe. The breakthrough of postmodern science revealed that what we had considered to be hard facts about the universe were really constructs of our own minds, created through our efforts to understand the world. The scientific viewpoint changed within the twentieth century from the mechanistic building blocks theory to a holistic view that admits the connectedness of the cosmos. Things are not static and boxable, but alive with movement, contrary to their apparent fixity. The so-called observer is not objectively detached, but is in a dynamic relationship with what he or she observes and even affects the observed object itself.

These scientific insights reminded me of something I had read long ago about how two people can have an effect upon each other just by being in the same room. The example given was that of two strangers in an art gallery. The author suggested that, even if the two people were concentrating on different paintings with their backs to each other and were on different sides of the room, they were nevertheless affected in some way by each other's presence, consciously or unconsciously. It seemed to be a non-rational experience, and perhaps neither person would ever reflect upon it or share the memory of it by telling a friend. It was an experience of mere presence, which demonstrated the dynamic nature of being.

Although I was reading in-depth material at this time, the works I came across explored the reality of everyday life, rather than leading the reader off into theoretical abstraction. One danger of living mostly in the mind is that we are prone to be absent to the reality of the present moment. Ken Wilber gives two vivid examples in *No Boundaries*. He compares our awareness of the present moment to a sandwich made with two of the thickest slices of bread imaginable. One slice is the past; the other is the future. The past and the future seem so real to us that "our present moment, the very meat of the sandwich, is reduced to a mere thin slice, so that our reality soon becomes all bread-ends with no filling." Then our minds constantly dwell in the past or the future, missing the only real moment—now. Wilber goes on to point out that what we call the past exists in reality as *present* memories, and what we call the future consists of *present* expectations. Constantly dwelling on these thoughts, we lose ourselves in our minds.

Rather than truly experiencing present reality, we attempt to "wave-jump," an activity that Wilber uses as another analogy. We think that this present moment is not acceptable or satisfying so we will not rest in it comfortably, but begin to imagine a more desirable present. "We begin…to wave-jump. We begin moving in space and time to secure for ourselves the ultimate wave, the wave that will finally quench our thirst, that will finally give us 'wetness.'" Wilber suggests that our preoccupation with the next experience precludes our being conscious of the present experience. We thus engage in an endless search, forever missing the now.

Wilber's analogy led me to reflect on my own preoccupation with urgently getting on with things. Moving past the present moment, instead of being in it, did seem to be most important. Making phone calls, correcting endless stacks of papers, going to the grocery store, "saying" prayers—all had to be done before I had time to be in the present moment, which never seemed to arrive, since these activities, once accomplished, had to be started all over again. Then there were the unsettling moments of losing something unfindable that the Borrowers must have snatched and hidden between the walls. Forgetting things, tripping over things—why did these things happen? Perhaps these "interruptions" were opportunities to stop, to be still, and to give up temporarily my feverish movement to be ahead of the present moment. And what about my impatience when waiting at a red light? Was it an overlooked opportunity to gaze up at the clouds for a moment or two? Take in some of the beauty around me? And to be thankful that at least we were all taking turns crossing the street? Ironically, it was stopping at a red light that gave me enough time to read a bumper sticker saying, "I'd rather be here now."

My trips to the wildflowers and walks at the lagoon were contemplative experiences that had helped ground me in the experience of the present moment through the senses. But I had found that the mind can also be a sacred path to present reality. As Evelyn Underhill writes, "Thought is a great and sacred force given to us by God, our share in the life that lies behind appearances." Only when thought is separated from reality does it leave the path of wisdom.

Eight

"Which Vice is Versa?"

It began to be clear to me that connectedness makes for wholeness and holiness, but that there is an important distinction to be made between true related unity and unconscious merging. We have to develop as individuals in order to relate consciously either to another person or to a group. Otherwise, we surrender to being mindlessly embedded in a collectivity. Such a choice, or perhaps just a gradual drifting toward a state of group thought or feeling, moves us toward a pseudo reality, a subtle form of evil. George MacDonald has written, "All wickedness tends to destroy individuality and declining natures assimilate as they sink."

Jesus uses the image of a narrow path or gate leading to his kingdom, indicative of an individual path. Putting it another way, E. E. Cummings writes, "The path is narrow to the right madness." Cummings implies that the right way is not only individual, but in some respect is beyond the limits of reason or logic. Jesus states that the way to perdition, on the other hand, is a wide path that many heedlessly follow. T. S. Eliot echoes this image in *The Cocktail Party*: "In a world of fugitives, the person taking the opposite direction will appear to be running away." The necessity of the individual journey is emphasized in the Arthurian legend of the Grail, in which each knight of the Round Table must make his own path into the forest, rather than following a trail created by someone else.

A number of authors have dealt with of the effects of unconscious merging. In *The Phantom Tollbooth*, Norton Jester points out the dangers of unthinking conformity when his hero, Milo, disregards the road signs and drives his little car into the Doldrums. This swamp-like place is the habitat of the Lethargians, creatures who follow a "strict schedule of daydreaming, napping, dawdling, delaying, lingering, loitering, loafing, lounging, dillydallying and procrastinating." Thinking, laughing, or doing anything is illegal. The Lethargians merge with their environment, taking on the colors of the things around them. Not only are they inactive, but they are indistinguishable, one from another. In the film version, they melt together, forming a morass that prevents Milo's car from moving and leaving him stuck in the Doldrums until the Watch Dog, who protects and values time, rescues him.

Madeline L'Engle presents a similar destructive force in *A Wrinkle in Time*. When Meg and her little brother Charles Wallace travel to the planet Camazotz, they find a collective brain referred to as It, which controls the inhabitants, who dress alike and live in identical houses. Meg's brother falls under the spell of It and surrenders his mind to the planet's group thought and action. Meg senses the danger and questions the devaluing of individuals on the planet. "It" answers her by pointing out that all are accepted and offered equality in that society. Speaking through her hypnotized brother, It tells her, "What we have on Camazotz [is] complete equality. Everybody exactly alike." After a moment of confusion, Meg sees the truth and blurts out, "No, …like and equal are not the same thing at all!" She saves her brother by continuing to love what she knows to be his unique self, even while he, under Its control, treats her with coldness and contempt. The one power that she has—that of love for an individual—proves to be stronger than the mesmerizing deceptions of It.

In his imagery of hell, George Bernanos, the French novelist, presents a terrifying picture of the unconscious merging that is the ultimate end of evil: "In the kingdom of evil what is truly central in the end is not at all the evil individual, but rather his [her] dissolution in the anonymity of flames and slime." His description of the Evil One is similar to Dante's Satan, who eternally chews upon three traitors in the pit of the Inferno. Bernanos writes, "What does the Monster care about one criminal more or less? On the spot he devours his crime, incorporates it into his frightful substance, and digests it without for a moment leaving his terrible, eternal immobility." In his conception of hell, or the state of evil, Bernanos depicts the fire that consumes those who radically choose evil as not only melting the perpetrators together, but as removing from them the ability to relate to one another: "The inconceivable misfortune of these glowing stones that once were humans is that they no longer have anything to share."

In *That Hideous Strength*, the third volume of his space trilogy, C. S. Lewis creates a tale in which a disembodied head, developed by the English scientists of N.I.C.E., becomes their master. Having put their trust in objective scientific theories, the scientists begin to worship the head and to follow its dictates. Unknown to them, the head is the mouthpiece of the Bent One (Satan) who desires complete rule over our planet. The work of the institute is directed toward the distortion of natural life on Earth. Its main projects include cruel experimentation on animals and the destruction of the woods, the natural streams, the flowers, etc., in order to build more laboratory space. Total control is the goal of the institute: "Quite simple and obvious things at first—sterilization of the unfit, liquidation of backward races, ...selective breeding. Then real education, including prenatal education...[that] makes the patient what it wants...psychological at first...on to biochemical conditioning in the end and direct manipulation of the brain." In other words, this Brain wants to control all other brains on earth, another example of unholy oneness.

Ken Wilber, in *A Brief History of Everything*, discusses the danger of preferring the collective way of objective fact over individuality and depth. He speaks of the "widespread loss of the spiritual in the West" as being caused by adopting a perspective that he calls "Flatland." The term implies that we have chosen to view only the external aspects or surfaces of reality. We see only "it," not "I" or "we." While L'Engle and Lewis present the image of a brain in fictional accounts, Wilber describes the brain as a scientific example to explain his theory. Although medical science can hook up a person's brain to a machine to study it, the physiologist "can know what every atom is doing, and he still won't know a single thought in my mind." In order to know what is in the patient's mind, the scientist must talk to the person. The author points out that certain aspects of reality have *interior* dimensions that "can only be accessed by communication and interpretation, by 'dialogue' and…approaches which are not *staring* at exteriors, but *sharing* of interiors. Not objective but intersubjective. Not surfaces but depth…. *Surfaces can be seen, but depth must be interpreted.*"

Wilber calls this view of surface reality the "monological gaze." He remarks that when a person gets a CAT scan of the brain, the technicians only talk to that person if they need to, for example, to ask her to move her position etc. He asks, "When the lab technicians take this objective picture of your brain, do they see the real you? Do they see *you* at all?" This monological gaze at a person as merely an object having no depth, not as a subject in communication is what makes the science of medicine dehumanizing. Wilber argues that where there is no awareness of depth, there is little consciousness. Increasing our awareness of depth increases our consciousness, through which the Spirit ultimately speaks to us.

Wilber's insights threw a great deal of light on my earlier questions about the bias that I had found in the educational field. The monological view had proclaimed that the interior depths requiring interpretation, as found in literature and other branches of the humanities, either didn't exist or just were not important. Hence the emphasis on the more objective subjects, such as science and math, and the objective approach to material that required a more subjective approach.

Flatland is a type of reductionism that encourages a mental merging in the sense that we are all supposedly seeing reality in the same way, having seen merely the surface. I had observed groups buying into the Flatland view, not only in educational institutions, but also in religious life, when much of the time was spent clarifying and reclarifying our positions on various issues and policies. Thomas Merton put it well: "communities are devoted to high-definition projects: making it all clear. The clearer it gets the more clear it has to be made. It branches out. You have to keep clearing the branches…. On the end of each branch there is a big bushy question mark." Institutions of almost any kind had begun placing undue emphasis on trying to pin down clearly in words what they were supposed to be doing rather than in worthwhile action.

The proliferation of words in meetings, in the media, and in political arenas gradually becomes a misuse, a disservice to real communication. Language itself is flattened out, losing depth and nuance, with the increasing preference for jargon. In *The Humiliation of the Word*, Jacques Ellul laments the disrespect for words in our technological society, one that puts more trust in visual images supplied globally through television. Alan Jones, in *Exploring Spiritual Direction* writes, "Jargon is a sin against intellectual chastity" He sees jargon as a prostitution of the purpose of language, i.e., to relate to one another through real communication. Harry Williams states that jargon "is an attempt to sound clever when you have nothing to say."

My reading told me that wholeness or holiness, in contrast to merging and superficial communication, entails individual personal development. Only when I become my real, unique self can I truly relate to others and to God. Looking back through some of my earlier notebooks I found a number of quotations from Socrates to Krishnamurti stating that true education is the understanding of oneself. A note from Yeats speaks of the "courage of entering into the abyss of one self" as requiring greater bravery than the exploration of any unknown territory. In a more recent work, Erich Neumann claims that the true "ethical task is to become conscious." All of these authors believed that true education must go beneath the surface and is ultimately a process of self exploration, not in a narcissistic mode of navel gazing, but in the sense of plumbing the depths of human experience.

However, it is necessary to explore the outer world first. On the old radio program called "Let's Pretend," there was a story about a boy and a girl who traveled around the world in search of the Blue Bird of Happiness, only to find it at last in their own backyard. Chesterton wrote a tale about a man who circled the globe in search of true happiness; he knew he had found it when he returned home to see his wife hanging up the clothes near the white picket fence of their home. The search must be undertaken, even though we may be led back to the place where we began, as T. S. Eliot writes, "When the last of earth left to discover is that which was the beginning." A person must grow and develop outwardly to a certain point before beginning the inner journey.

Because we are called to growth and development throughout our lives, one aspect of personal sin is the refusal to mature. James Finley once gave the example of a poster picturing a baby chicken newly hatched; the caption read "What now?" In the case of the chick, he pointed out, the answer was simple: Eat. We, on the other hand, have to choose to become human, a process that entails more than eating. Frances Wickes, in *The Inner World of Choice*, uses examples from her casework in psychotherapy that show children's experiences in making early choices between good and evil. An eight-year-old girl created an ugly beast out of clay. When questioned about it, she said that she had seen the beast in a dream and that she sometimes talked to the clay image. One day she asked the beast, "Are you young or old?" He answered, "I am very, very old, yet you are my mother." The girl described the beast as being her best friend, and an ally against anyone that asked too hard a task of her. Wickes comments, "The beast was child of her own desire to destroy any force that opposed her will. The desire, as old as human life, was reborn through her choice of alliance with its potential in herself…in order to kill the demands life makes."

Wickes believes that evil, "may be born anew—within a child by almost unconscious choice, yet it is a choice." She gives another example, this one of a timid, lazy boy who avoided homework and energetic companions. He liked to drift into the land of daydreams, floating on the "Lotus Island of somnolent content." Wickes describes this island: "Here the crocodile god, Inertia, presides. He invites you to share his sunny log and, as you contentedly bask in the sun, he obligingly swallows the energy that might disturb your sleep." Wickes sees inertia as one of the most deadly enemies of conscious choice. But through our own positive choices, God gives us the power to confront evil. She writes, "The act of grace and the act of choice establish a covenant between man and God."

A principal in one of the high schools where I taught slipped a pamphlet into each of the faculty members' mail slots in the mid 1980s. It included an allegory about two butterfly parents eagerly awaiting the birth of their cocoon-encased baby and dreaming of all that their little butterfly would accomplish, etc. When the time came, their darling peeked out, looked around, and said, "It's really comfortable in here—I think I'll just stay here and hang around with you, Mom and Dad." At the time, this example of adolescent inertia illustrated well the growing tendency of high schoolers to merely join the ranks of the unemployed following graduation, rather than to move on with their lives, establishing themselves through a career choice, etc.

George Bernanos comments strongly on the consequences of refusing to grow, to act, to choose: "Won't damnation be the tardy discovery, the discovery much too late, after death, of a soul absolutely unused, still carefully folded together, and spoiled, the way precious silks are spoiled when they are not used?" And Jesus had nothing good to say about the man in the parable who buried his talent out of fear. The inherent call of each individual to work toward personal development is also sounded at the beginning of the book of Genesis. Wilkie Au tells the story of a rabbi who asked his students why the Bible states "God saw that it was good" after each day of creation *except* the sixth day, when humans were created. Was it because humans are not good? Au explains that the Hebrew word used for "good" is *tov*, a word that can be translated as "complete." The implication is that, unlike the rest of creation, humans are not born complete, but must grow and develop in order to fulfill their destiny by making choices that lead to psychological and spiritual maturity.

But what, then, about original sin? It seemed that I had been led back to my initial questions about the subject. I had already concluded that the idea of a single act of disobedience in the past, punished by the universal curse of original sin, must be a literal reading of a symbolic truth. To literalize is to idolize, in certain situations. For example, while Moses was speaking to the invisible God on the mountain, his people chose to build their own literal god out of gold. It was easier for them to see a golden calf before them, than to confront the deep mystery of God.

The notion of dire consequences resulting from a single act was familiar to me as a Catholic child. We were taught that if we ate meat on Friday once or failed to attend Sunday Mass, we would be sent to hell if we died shortly thereafter without having confessed these mortal sins. I remember visiting with friends of my parents who didn't attend Mass regularly. They were a kind, friendly couple, and as I sat there listening to the lively conversation filled with laughter, I wondered how they could be so cheerful when they were obviously on shaky ground with God. The logic behind such beliefs was like the game I had played on the way to school, trying not to step on cracks, and imagining the dreadful things that might happen to me if my resolve weakened or my foot slipped.

A number of other authors have attempted to throw light upon the idea of original sin. M. Scott Peck equates original sin with laziness—a tendency similar to Wickes' examples of being tempted by inertia. Peck points out that evil is opposed to life and growth and notes that "EVIL" is "LIVE" spelled backwards. Alan Jones writes that one consequence of the Fall is self-contemplation, an act in which we turn our gaze back upon ourselves in a narcissistic fashion. Thomas Merton paints a similar picture. He describes the Fall as Adam's falling inward into himself: "Adam had passed through the center of himself and emerged on the other side to escape from God by putting himself between himself and God." Sebastian Moore sees original sin as the "withdrawing into isolated self-awareness of man from the mystery on which he depends." He writes of this sin as "the systematic reduction of the child of mystery to the banal world of man's own making." Bernanos echoes Wilber's idea of Flatland's tendency to ignore the depths and only acknowledge the surfaces of reality when he writes, "Sin is always a lie. The very essence of the sinner…is his refusal to engage the full depth of his being and make it something vital: at base, the sinner is someone who lives at the surface of himself."

Another attribute ascribed to original sin is willfulness. Donald Mitchell, an expert on Christian/Buddhist studies writes, "this dissatisfactory condition of original sin is like a darkness in which one is unable to see his or her original nature in God at the Center of one's being…. The blind willfulness to be and to possess darkens human life so that people cannot recognize…the presence, beauty, compassion and loving activity of God." Moore believes that through our willfulness "the ego crucifies the self." Reflecting upon these authors' insights, I concluded that original sin, rather than being something we could blame on Adam and Eve, seemed to be more in the nature of an inside job.

Perhaps a profound fear of freedom underlies our sinful condition. Northrope Frye, near the end of his book on the Bible and literature entitled *The Great Code*, throws further light on the subject. He writes that the doctrine of original sin "holds that since the fall of Adam, human life has been cursed with a built-in inertia that will forever prevent man from fulfilling his destiny without divine help." He suggests that it is really more accurate to think of original sin as the fear we have of freedom and a resistance to responsibility and discipline that it demands. He states that freedom is the most important thing that the gospel has to offer, but that we do not naturally want the freedom God wants to give us. What we really want is "to collapse back into the master-slave duality." Frye's remarks reminded me of the Grand Inquisition's scene in *The Brothers Karamozov*; Jesus is condemned to death because he offers the people freedom. One Fourth of July, I attended a Mass at which the celebrant gave a homily that referred to this passage from Dostovesky's novel. The priest ended by stating that people don't want to be free; they want to be safe and right. But of course, Jesus never indicated that the truth will make us safe.

The refusal of God's offer of freedom is in reality the choice to remain children in a world of external authority, rather than to grow up to be adult children of God. This choice places us in a world that tells us it is bad to question, but good to conform. It is better to follow rules than to listen to the Spirit within. Stepping out of the collective world creates enough neurotic guilt in us to discourage such a move, thereby encouraging the preference to remain safe and right, rather than to be freed. The bind it puts most people in is bad enough, but what further inhibits a move toward freedom are the inner voices of pseudo authority, inner enemies of which we are unaware. These voices come from internalized parental voices and complexes that operate unconsciously within us. Listening to these voices, we as adults make choices that prevent us from hearing or responding to the freedom offered us as the sons and daughters of God. Like the children's choices presented in Wickes' examples, our choices may be made almost unconsciously, but are still choices. Because of a certain degree of unconsciousness, these negative choices seem to be somehow in-born and therefore feel as if they were being directed by natural tendencies beyond our control, similar to the idea of the sinful tendencies inherited through original sin.

Looking through some of my notebooks once more, I found a variety of insights along the same lines. Northrope Frye writes, "sin is not illegal or antisocial behavior, but rather a matter of trying to block the activity of God, and it always results in some curtailing of freedom, whether of oneself or one's neighbor." George MacDonald states, "The one thing that cannot be forgiven is the sin of...refusing deliverance. It is impossible to forgive that. It would be to take part in it." MacDonald here is interpreting Jesus' teaching that all sins will be forgiven, except the sin against the Holy Spirit, which is the refusal to accept the truth of the Spirit's offer to free us from sin. Gandhi supports the idea of the existence of internal enemies within ourselves by stating, "The only devils are the ones in our own hearts. That is where the battle should be fought." James Hollis refers to the two grinning gremlins of Lethargy and Despair that sit at the foot of our beds each morning, gladly waiting to devour us if we are not alert. He comments that, no matter how we handled these demons yesterday, we must confront them again daily, especially in middle-age.

One of the most frightening aspects of our present world is the constant escalation of deadly acts of violence, perpetrated in a number of instances even by children. Lawrence Jaffe, a Jungian analyst, compares the infamy of the Holocaust with our unconscious inner tendencies to inflict violence on ourselves. He notes that the Nazis attempted to rid the world of a people upon whom they projected their own fear, weakness, and imperfection. He remarks that if we, in the present day take up arms to rid our world of "Nazis," then we are embarking on the same kind of violence that the Nazis themselves carried out, supposedly attempting to rid the world of evil. He suggests that we look to the enemy within, saying, "Listen to this: a Nazi is alive in your heart." Jaffe indicates that our inner Nazi is out to get our most wounded, vulnerable parts, and to destroy our "inner Jew." He describes her: "she is weak, wounded. Seek her out. Take her in your arms, listen to her troubles. When the inferior is accepted, when what falls short is accepted, the

Nazi is starved and weakened." The proud ego in us desires to irradicate all imperfections—all those things that we think will not be approved of or accepted by others. What we don't realize is that we need to accept these weak imperfect parts of ourselves. On one level our willingness to do so will warrant Jesus' affirmation, "What you have done to these, the least of my brethren, you have done to me." Accepting what we consider the least aspect of ourselves may be considerably more difficult than being kind to others.

The attempt to seek out and destroy the most vulnerable parts of ourselves is encouraged by the inner enemy, who, having interjected parental and societal voices, tells us that we must be perfect and successful in all things. We must bring home a straight A report card in all subjects. In a success-oriented culture, efforts in this direction might seem to be working toward growth and development, but are really forms of sabotage.

However, any personification of a destructive exterior force might very well be a projection of our inner Nazi, who tries to control and manipulate our inner sensitivities and vulnerabilities. One method of control used to keep all the unmanageable aspects of life in line is to put one's faith solely in logic or reason. Bernanos writes, "the logic of evil is as strict as hell. The devil is the greatest of logicians or perhaps, who knows, he may be logic itself." Chesterton presents a similar view, but in a more matter of fact, English style, "The madman is not the man who has lost his reason. The madman is the man who has lost everything except his reason...his mind moves all the quicker for not being delayed by the things that go with good judgment. He is not hampered by sense of humor or by charity or by the dumb certainties of experience. If you argue with a madman it is extremely probable that you will get the worst of it."

To put our entire trust in reason and logic is to make a choice to live in Flatland, on the surface of reality. It is an attempt to reduce the complexity and depth of life to a simple surface that can be completely understood and therefore controlled. We cannot control the shadow and our inner voices by will power or reason. They appear in our dreams or erupt in our bursts of anxiety, anger or fear, etc. If we try too hard to suppress them, they visit us in states of depression or physical illness. Only by becoming conscious enough to be aware of them and to attempt to integrate them can we move toward wholeness/holiness. We may not then always be safe and right, but will develop the disposition to receive the freedom of the sons and daughters of God offered us by the Spirit.

Through reflective listening, meditation, and attention, we can begin to hear those inner voices that may be questionable, and to balance them with the real voice of the true inner self. Jung's helpful theory is that the conscious self must watch and listen for unconscious voices and tendencies to emerge. Then, rather than taking sides with either voice, the task is to bear the tension of the opposites within oneself until a transformative third way appears—an attitude that in some way integrates and incorporates both in a healing, psychological and spiritual balance. An example of this process might be found in the story of Abraham, who carried the tension between his obedience to Yahweh and his love for his son up the mountain until the angel revealed to him an alternative sacrifice, a ram hiding in the brush. The same attitude is appropriate for taking a matter for discernment to prayer to wait it out in order to hear the voice of the Spirit above all the conflicting sounds within or without. In outer life, it is often the place of the Christian to stand in the middle between two conflicting groups, as a reconciling presence, rather than to further the conflict by taking sides. And in the educational field, the attitude of conscious listening is most important. Simone Weil emphasized this skill, even stating that the main purpose of education is to develop the capacity for attention, since that is what prayer essentially demands.

The cross itself is a symbol of enduring the crucifying tension of opposites. Something new is born through the suffering of the experience. A new attitude that unites the disparate fragments of ourselves and the world is resurrected from the willingness to undergo the tension. Hence Jesus' statement that we are to take up our cross daily in order to become like him by following him as the Way. The Good News in this context is not that, because of Jesus' sacrifice, we can be transformed by Baptism into a pure state in which all we have to do is to avoiding stepping on cracks, to let nothing trail in the mud, to wash regularly and then to hope we can make it into heaven by staying clean. Jesus does not save us from our own experience, but shows the truth of the way to live as he did. The way out is the living through whatever tension or conflict each experience brings.

Ann Ulanov, in her book, *The Transcendent Function*, describes the psychological work we must do in order to become whole enough to listen to the voice of the Spirit within. She refers to "what Jung calls our religious instinct, that open-ended connection to something beyond us that really knows about us…. It is our [positive] ego work to re-collect all that was ever ours, the good as well as the bad, to claim and own and sense in our body that this is who we are and where we stand." By a self-acceptance won through the help of the Spirit, we allow ourselves to be healed of our inner divisiveness and fragmentation.

Jesus was a living example of wholeness, showing us the way by incarnating it. In *Jesus the Therapist*, Hanna Wolff describes the manner in which Jesus dealt with the opposites in his life: "First of all we have the following poles in tension: *uncompromising certitude* and *receptive openness.* Jesus is never the man of the 'On the one hand…on the other hand.' He takes a position, and demands his fellow human beings do likewise." He states clearly that we are to say a very simple yes or no, indicating that further words are from the evil one. Secondly, Hanna remarks that, as evidenced by his openness in dealing with a particular Samaritan woman, Jesus' attitude is not one of rigidity or narrowness, following the collective rejection of her group that was practiced by his people. Jesus' attitude rather suggests that hesitation and wishy-washiness in respect to one's own position have never accomplished anything positive. The tendency toward ambivalence in everything can eventually lead to the moral relativism, so prevalent today.

Reflecting upon the healing process released by holding the tension of the opposites psychologically and spiritually, I began to see the underlying reason that I had always felt that language itself, well used, holds a spiritual dimension. Robert Johnson, in *Owning Your Shadow*, claims that "to make any well formed sentence is to make unity out of duality [and]…is immensely healing and restorative. We are all poets and healers when we use language correctly." He uses as an example T. S. Eliot's line from *The Four Quartets*: "The fire and the rose are one." Johnson compares the structure of the sentence to a mathematical equation, the verb standing in the place of the equal sign and annulling the "the split inherent in duality." I had used a similar comparison in teaching grammar: metaphors have a particularly healing effect, liberating us from Flatland statements about the surface of reality. Frances Wickes put it well, "The hollow man speaks more than he says, but the living man bears the voice of the Great Spirit—he speaks in myth and poetry." Language well used, metaphor in particular,—can help us to turn the fragmentation of an either/or world into a more integrated both/and world.

I wondered if language better used would have helped out in many of the fruitless meetings that I had attended through the years, which failed to reach a workable synthesis or integration of the diverse points of view of the people who attended them. Often a solution that really pleased no one, or a nonsolution that just left things as they were before the meeting was the unsatisfactory outcome. We failed to connect, to relate to each other enough to produce a creative plan of action. Therefore, endless equally fruitless follow-up meetings were scheduled, but were carried on in the same mode of unconnectedness, which left us pretty much back at square one.

An extreme example of either/or thinking is found in one of the Pogo cartoon strips entitled "Which Vice is Versa?" Owl and Churchy the turtle are discussing the problem of air pollution. Owl had read an article in the swamp newspaper written by a woman who claimed that "air pollution hurts people just as much as smokin'…everybody got to have *one* vice." Churchy asks, "What's hers? Smokin'?" Owl answers, "No, I think it's breathin'." He then reflects upon the facts that people sit indoors and breathe next to the polluting chimneys that warm them; they take smog-producing cars into the country side to breathe fresh air, and they smoke cigars, an activity that requires breathing. He then concludes, waving his turtle fist in the air, "You want to cut down air pollution? Cut down the original source—BREATHIN'."

The two discuss the matter further, considering how people might at least cut down on one or the other of the activities required for breathing—either inhaling or exhaling. Churchy arrives at a third idea that would simplify the problem further and blurts out: "It's the inhalin' and exhalin' that *causes* trouble. People should do one or the other—NOT BOTH!" This strip of Walt Kelly's seemed to satirize well the tendency to the either/or sort of dualistic thinking that leads nowhere. The irony in the cartoon is that air pollution *was* originally caused by "breathin"—that is, by breathing human beings who created the technology that produced all the pollutants. Needless to say, Pogo's friends just dropped the issue and walked on through the swamp in search of other adventures.

Nine

Full Circle

Self-discipline is an important trait to develop when one is growing up, but it can become an obstacle to the surrender of self necessary to respond to God's freeing graces later in life. Putting all of our trust in self-control can lead to making an idol of perfectionism. In other words, we become devoted to the project of creating a bigger, better "me" or egocentric self. David Richo in his book, *When Love Meets Fear*, states directly, "The only obstacle to grace…is control." The spiritual life, meant to free us from our preoccupation with ourselves, can turn into just another form of self-obsession. Although I never appreciated the rigid asceticism proposed by Rodriguez, his story about the monk who hung a sausage in his cell during Lent to test his asceticism and then ate it on Good Friday held a wise insight.

In the early 1960s I had been struck by a statement of Josef Goldbrunner's concerning what it means to become a saint. He wrote, "When the ideal of holiness represents the sum of all virtues, a lifeless plaster image is set up, and the striving for holiness becomes mere imitation. The real starting point should be the individual." To fall for the idea/idol of perfection is to set ourselves up for certain failure, and then inevitably get a beating from our inner idealist. The thesis of his book is summed up in his title: *Holiness is Wholeness*.

The problem in making choices that lead to wholeness/holiness is that the false self, the egocentric ego, opposes the growth of the true self, the heir of heaven, the daughter or son of God. Even if we accomplish great good in the world, our unconscious shadow may trick us into believing that we are perfect and then betray us if we are not aware. A good example might be that of Gandhi, the man of nonviolence, who showed the world how violence can be stopped by a brave person who is willing to absorb the blow of an enemy without returning it. His extreme personal ascetical practices became forms of inner violence that eventually caused upsets and rifts between him and his closest followers.

Since even our best moral efforts will not make us perfect, it is no wonder that we tend to fall into discouragement and negative thoughts about ourselves as we become more enlightened as to our true situation. Ironically, becoming more conscious gives rise to the temptation to turn against ourselves. But negative thoughts of any kind can cause fragmentation and disease. Jung suggested that the gods worshipped by the ancient world seem to have disappeared, but in reality have become the diseases that visit us—making us uneasy, putting us in a state of disease, either physically or psychologically. In this view, when we have a disease, we are really experiencing the visitation of a messenger who is trying to make us aware of something important that we need to look at in our lives. Striving for the ego ideal of perfection may be one of the most effective ways to bring illnesses upon ourselves, since we are really working against our basic human condition, rather than choosing the path of growth that leads to wholeness.

Jung wrote that there is an undeveloped potential in our shadow qualities comparable to undiscovered gold. Our rejection of ourselves because of our unacceptable imperfections just makes us more miserable, deaf to messengers and warning signs. Unconscious, repressed, unintegrated attitudes hold an unused energy that can be tapped and turned into sources of growth. Massimilla and Bud Harris, in *Like Gold Through Fire*, tell us that "It is in our faults and our deformities that our salvation lies, where we are wounded and where we have stumbled that we find the psychological gold that holds the key to new development. The seeds of transformation and new life generally reside in the areas we have rejected and secretly fear." Fortunately there is a redemptive element present in the shadow activity perpetrated by unconscious energies that can be brought to light, turned to positive uses, and developed into abilities we perhaps have only seen in others, but were unaware of as potentials in ourselves.

This work of reconciliation within ourselves is an example of Jung's theory of the healing third dimension. It is a form of holding the tension between two seeming opposites: for example, the negative trait I see in myself, and my growing realization of its positive possibilities. The gold we discover in our shadow qualities can act as the transcendent third way. In the story of St. George, the dragon might be considered to be a symbol of the shadow. After the hero slays the dragon, he and the villagers cut up the shadow beast and eat it, thereby finding nourishment in what they had considered to be totally evil. Robert Johnson remarks in one of his works that the killing of the dragon shouldn't be the end of the story about St. George. He suggests that probably both George and the dragon were injured in the fight. But the story, to be one of healing, should include compassion for the dragon, who should be befriended and nursed back to health. The restored dragon might then gift us with some of its well-guarded treasures, as the accepted shadow side yields its gold.

In Matthew's gospel Jesus tells his followers to love their enemies: "Do not resist one who is evil. But if anyone strikes you on the right cheek, turn to him the other also.... Do good to those who hate you, bless those who curse you. Do not be overcome by evil, but overcome evil with good." These exhortations are obviously meant to direct our attention to the inherent good in others, even in our enemies, but the most difficult enemy to love is ourselves in our weakness, vulnerability, and imperfection.

When we grow strong enough to acknowledge and accept our imperfections, our inner demons' possession and control over us lessens. Alan Jones writes, "Giving up our low opinion of ourselves (the last trick of the ego to keep us concentrated on ourselves)" is essential to living an authentic spiritual life. We must be willing to bear the burden of our own emotions—to feel them and learn from them, rather than to act them out or repress them. Accepting the truth of our situation requires that we see ourselves as neither worse nor better than we actually are. St. Therese of Lisieux tells us, "If you are willing to serenely bear the trial of being displeasing to yourself, then you will be for Jesus a pleasant place of shelter." She must have taken her own advice, since she later reveals, "Nowadays I am resigned to seeing myself in a state of permanent imperfection, and I delight in it."

In offering hospitality to the vulnerable parts of ourselves we need to let go of the drive to control, and also the tendency to avoid mistaking worry, anxiety, and fear for virtues to be regularly exercised. In casting our cares upon the Lord we choose to trust ourselves to God's providence. Walter Kerr refers to "the frisky escape from the drive toward automated perfection" so needed in our technologically controlled world. When we are able to hold the tension of the unknowns in our lives—what Keats referred to as "negative capability"—unexpected helpful energies emerge from within ourselves and in the world around us, offering themselves to us through our openness to receive them.

In the Christian scheme of redemption, Jesus does not save us from our particular circumstances, but is our model for entering into the depth of our experience and suffering through its challenges so as to become transformed into a new mode of living. The bearing of the cross of our own experience, following Jesus' example, demonstrates that we truly believe his words. Looking back through my own experience, I had found examples of the pattern I had discovered to be true of the human experience for everyone. The mysterious, but necessary journey begins by moving out into the world, seeking for the Bluebird of Happiness, only to find it at last in our own backyard, as do the children in the story. If the journey is a spiritual search, the temptation prompted by our technological world is to buy a Build-It-Yourself Saint Kit and follow the directions, only to find that the self-built model is artificial and lifeless. We must then return "to our own backyard" by undertaking a journey to the kingdom within, where after all our striving, we hope to hear the words spoken to the pilgrim in Frances Thompson's poem: "All that your heart's desire fancied as lost/I have stored for you at home."

When I was growing up, priests came yearly to our parish to preach a mission. For several days the talks focused on the repentance of sins. Many of the sermons were of the hell, fire, and damnation variety. Years later I read James Joyce's *Portrait of the Artist as a Young Man.* Joyce must have heard a number of these sermons himself, for he creates one in which the preacher describes the horror and tortures of hell in such detail that its length makes the reader wonder if it will ever end. The purpose of such a sermon seemed to be to frighten people into repentance, in case they had no higher motivation. By the time I read Joyce's novel, I had begun to question the logic of preaching mainly about damnation instead of proclaiming the Good News of the gospel.

More recently I came across Carol Lee Flinders' book on seven women mystics, entitled *Enduring Grace.* The revelations of Julian of Norwich hold consoling insights that contrast with the hell and damnation approach. Flinders writes of Julian, "Sin was the problem. Holy Church seemed to say one thing, the God of her revelations another." The church teachings had given the visionary the idea that most of us are such great sinners that God in his just wrath will necessarily condemn huge numbers of us to eternal punishment. Having questioned God in prayer about her confusion, Julian was granted a number of revelations that took her a lifetime to reflect upon. One of her visions has to do with God's loving attitude toward all of creation. The whole of creation appears to her as a sphere the size of a hazelnut. It seems too small to even exist but the voice of her vision tells her, "It lasts and always will, because God loves it; and thus everything has being through the love of God." The hazelnut universe of creation reminded me of William Blake's lines about seeing "heaven in a wild flower" and "the world in a grain of sand." The size of a created being does not prevent it from being a revelation of the Creator. The presence of the Creator who sustains them is inherent in all things. Eckhart surprisingly chooses the lowly fly as an example: "If you take [consider] a fly in God, it is in God far nobler than the highest angel in itself."

Acceptance of our paradoxical situation as created beings with limitations and imperfections, yet fashioned in the image of God as his sons and daughters, is the challenge facing us. Recently I was sitting in a waiting room with a woman who teaches in a religious education program in her parish. She told me about a retreat day that her team had made at a house of prayer. The directors had made quite an impression on her group with the story of the origin of the place, which they claimed had come about through prayer, faith, and then acceptance of the gift of the house, given in answer to prayer. "I was really impressed," she said. "I usually turn to God as a last resort." Her candid remark touched a guilty nerve in me, as it might in many of us who profess to be about God's work, but fall into the delusion that we are solely responsible and capable of operating on our own. William Barry states that one of Ignatius of Loyola's dictums, "Pray as if everything depended on God; work as if everything depended on you" is really a misinterpretation. The more accurate rendition is, "Pray as if everything depended on you; work as if everything depended on God." In other words, we can do our best, but it is always a limited best, and the effect or success is up to God.

Acceptance of ourselves brings us peace and allows us to rest in the truth of humility. During the time set aside for prayer, this acceptance extends to our being content even with our inability to remain present and attentive in prayer. For the struggle to give up our compulsions to control and direct ourselves and our world is an ongoing challenge. We may feel many times like the anonymous speaker in a poem that I copied down years ago in a notebook:

> Never again shall I walk under the star of my eyes
> And on the staff of my strength.
> You have torn away my shores,
> You have done violence to the earth under my feet.
>
> My ships are drifting out to sea—
> You have cut all their moorings
> The chains of my thoughts are broken,
> They hang wild over the deep.

Perseverance in prayerfully placing ourselves in the presence of God, gradually allowing grace to work upon our compulsions, may sometimes result in consolation. At these times we may feel ourselves to be who we truly are—in Charles Williams' words "one of the living creatures that run about and compose the web of glory."

Experiences of this kind may then be followed by dryness or darkness. When we remain responsive to God's presence in the world in dark times, we may identify with the speaker in "The Hound of Heaven" by Francis Thompson:

> I dimly guess what time in mists confounds,
> Yet ever and anon a trumpet sounds
> From the hid battlements of Eternity.
> Those shaken mists a space unsettle, then
> Round the half-glimpsed turrets slowly wash again.

We experience moments of light, followed by those of darkness, alternating experiences that shape the pattern of our lives. We struggle, as T. S. Eliot puts it, "to recover what has been lost/and found and lost again."

This alternating pattern is to be accepted as part of our human condition. When we experience consolation and light, we may be tempted to think we have achieved something, in which case, the aftermath of the experience feels like regression. The important thing is being present in the moment, whatever it brings.

For me, the best practice for entering into the present has been stopping my frenzied activities long enough to listen, to look, and to be in the moment. This is the approach taken in the contemplative type of prayer session, but can also be a way of pausing for a few minutes during a busy day. In *Spirit of Shaolin*, David Carradine has included a chapter on meditation in which he quotes Confucius: "Some…have hit the true center, and then? A very few have been able to stay there. The process is not understood. The men of talent shoot past it, and the others do not get to it." Carradine applies the statement to the practice of the type of centering prayer that is of a contemplative nature. However, it seems that Confucius' statement might also be true of finding a balance in life between contemplation and action.

Taking time to stop, to rest, to pray, to allow God to take over requires more self-discipline the more we have given our lives to ceaseless work and activity. It entails a certain death to egocentric demands. Some people become so desperate in the attempts to control their lives and the world around them that they are tempted to thoughts of suicide. Robert Johnson's advice to one of his clients who felt this way was, "It's all right to commit suicide, as long as you don't harm yourself physically in anyway." The advice suggests that giving up our attempted control of the universe can feel like a death, but perhaps it is a death similar to that referred to in another saying from Confucius:

He who knows he has enough is rich.
To die but not to perish
Is to be eternally present.
One must know when to stop.

Unfortunately, even prayer can become just one more thing that we do. Having acknowledged its importance, we may schedule it into our lives and carry it out as one more activity. But not even prayer is something we can accomplish by ourselves. Beatrice Bruteau states "Prayer is the work of God within us.... The deepest part of our consciousness knows that we live in eternity." Even in prayer, we must ultimately go with the flow and let God transform us. In contemplative prayer we let go of the controls, becoming like the leaf in one of Carradine's examples: "The position of the leaf that drifts effortlessly through the rapids is precisely correct at all times." This attitude, taken in prayer and in life as well, puts us in touch with the eternal purposes of God, which can only be fulfilled in the reality of the present moment.

Each moment deserves attention and must be lived courageously, especially when our feelings are at a low ebb or when nothing seems to be happening. These are times to listen even more intently for small stirrings, clues beckoning us to true obedience, which is a listening response to the voice of the Spirit in all things, the seemingly insignificant as well as the dramatic. T. S. Eliot describes our ordinary experience:

> For most of us, there is only the unattended
> Moment, the moment in and out of time,
> The distraction fit, lost in a shaft of sunlight,
> The wild thyme unseen, or the winter lightning
> Or the waterfall, or music heard so deeply
> That it is not heard at all, but you are the music
> While the music lasts...
> The hint half guessed, the gift half understood, is incarnation.

The term "incarnation" refers not only to Jesus, but also to us. If the Spirit dwells within us, we need to grow out of an attitude that sees authority as existing only outside ourselves, to be handed down to us in the form of preconceived ideas and rigid formulas based on the experiences of others. "For the pattern is new in every moment," Eliot writes. If we are truly open to the experience of the moment, we can then give a personal response. The word "response" is derived from Latin and Greek roots meaning "to promise in return," "to answer," "to betroth," and even "to pour a libation." It shares the same roots as the word "spouse." To be open to the present moment is to be attentive to God's presence in the form that present experience takes. This attentiveness itself becomes an act of prayer, hence Paul's exhortation, "Pray always."

Prayer seen from this perspective is not an isolated, individual action, as in something that we do separately. Its relational aspect mirrors the image and activity of God. Elizabeth Johnson sees the symbol of the Trinity as representing a community of equals and the divine life as a relationship that circulates, exchanging life and energy in a round dance that is eternal. To relate consciously to God, our true center, is to join in some way this dance of God. We are all invited to join in, and thereby are all united with each other on a profound level by accepting the invitation. Even so, because of our human limitations, we may experience our oneness only in rare moments. Much of the time our experience is like that described in a verse from Edward Markham:

> We all dance around
> In a ring and suppose
> But the Secret sits in the middle
> And knows.

The Secret is the mystery of God's presence within us, which ultimately connects us all to one another through the reality of this indwelling. Taking some time each day to empty ourselves of our busy preoccupations in receptive, contemplative prayer allows the Secret to speak. Rather than separating us from others, this centering prayer calls us also to relate to others in service and compassion. In this way we ourselves carry out the round dance of God in the world. Although we are called to bring about the realization of God's kingdom through service and compassion, all of our efforts then lead us back to the contemplation of God.

In the backyard of the house where I now live, there is a beautiful old tree with sky blue blossoms. I had never seen one like it, and found out from a local nursery that it is an Australian skyflower tree. Recovering from a severe case of shingles, I began sitting outside under the tree, unable to do much but gaze up into it. Although in my early sixties, I felt as drained of energy as if I were much older. Glancing at an essay by Helen Luke, I noted her comment that the "proper occupations of old age" are prayer, song, the telling of old tales, and laughter. She writes, "All these four things are activities *without purpose*, any one of them immediately killed by any hint of striving for achievement. They come to birth only in a heart freed from preoccupation with the goals of ego, however 'spiritual' or lofty these goals may be." She adds that this does not mean that we become unconcerned about the world as we age. Instead she advocates King Lear's suggestion that we "take upon us the mystery of things, as if we were God's spies."

During my recuperation I began to delve into some of the things that had been mysterious to me, writing about them under the skyflower tree. One of the first that came to mind was the notion of original sin. Looking back at my own spy job, it seems that the condition of original sin is one in which we are unaware of God's invitation to the Dance. We imagine ourselves to be alone, alienated, outside the Dance, when all the time the Dance continues within us and around us. It is in coming to the consciousness that we are in and of the Incarnation that frees us from this blindness.

As we weave in and out of the Dance, alternating between action and contemplation, we become more aware of our connection with God, with others, and with the world. Each moment is just what it is meant to be. As I end this book where it began, under the tree from Down Under, I recall T. S. Eliot's lines, "Quick now, here, now always—ridiculous the sad time/stretching before and after." And I add a verse of my own to celebrate this particular moment, before moving on:

> This is the holiest place to be,
> Watching the birds in the skyflower tree
> And letting them watch me.

0-595-33664-7

CPSIA information can be obtained
at www.ICGtesting.com
Printed in the USA
FSHW020228160720
72052FS